SNIP-AND-TELL BIBLE STORIES

BY
KARYN HENLEY

Group®
Loveland, Colorado

Group resources actually work!

This Group resource incorporates our R.E.A.L. approach to ministry. It reinforces a growing friendship with Jesus, encourages long-term learning, and results in life transformation, because it's

Relational
Learner-to-learner interaction enhances learning and builds Christian friendships.

Experiential
What learners experience through discussion and action sticks with them up to 9 times longer than what they simply hear or read.

Applicable
The aim of Christian education is to equip learners to be both hearers and doers of God's Word.

Learner-based
Learners understand and retain more when the learning process takes into consideration how they learn best.

Snip-and-Tell Bible Stories

Visit our website: **group.com**

Credits

Edited by Jennifer Root Wilger
Interior designed by Dori Walker
Cover designed by Liz Howe
Cover photography by David Priest
Illustrations by Jan Knudson

Library of Congress Cataloging-in-Publication Data

Henley, Karyn.
    Snip and tell Bible stories / by Karyn Henley.
        p.   cm.
    ISBN 978-1-55945-192-5
    1. Bible stories, English. 2. Christian education—Audio-visual aids. I. Title.
    BS551.2.H47   1993
    220.9'505—dc20   92-42492
                                                                        CIP

29 28 27 26 25   16 15 14 13 12
Printed in the United States of America.

CONTENTS

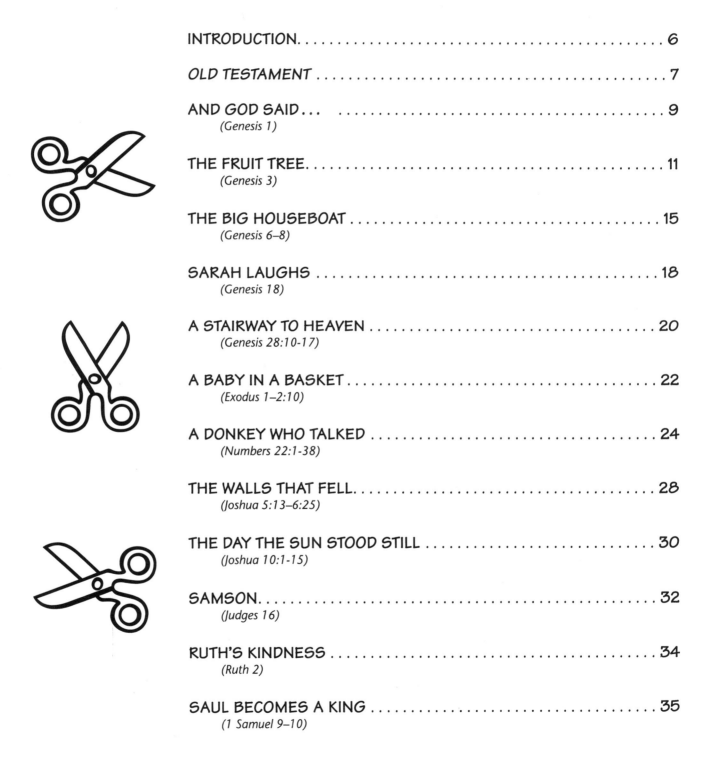

INTRODUCTION

Jesus says, "Every teacher...is like the owner of a house who brings out of his storeroom new treasures as well as old" (Matthew 13:52, NIV). *Snip-and-Tell Bible Stories* is designed to help tellers of Bible stories add new treasures to their storehouses of methods. Use these "treasures" to supplement your Sunday school or children's church materials, during a children's message time, or even for bedtime stories at home.

Snip-and-Tell Bible Stories will capture your students' attention with fascinating visual aids you create yourself. Each Bible story is accompanied by a photocopiable pattern for you to fold and cut as you talk. Each figure you create will depict an important element of the Bible story. Your Jonah will be swallowed by a huge fish, your David will fell the giant, and your Zacchaeus will climb down from the tree! Any story you choose will come to life as you snip and tell.

Here are a few tips for using the stories:

● **Practice.** Become familiar with the story you'll be telling. Photocopy practice patterns on plain or scratch paper. Practice telling the story as you fold and cut the figure. Unless the instructions tell you otherwise, always follow the dotted lines for folding and the solid lines for cutting.

● **Prepare.** Remove the story you've chosen from the book by tearing along the perforated edges. Copy the patterns for the story onto the sheet of paper you want to use. If you're using construction paper, transfer the pattern by using carbon paper or by tracing an imprint of the pattern onto your paper. To create an imprint, place your construction paper underneath the pattern and draw firmly over the pattern with a pencil. The imprint will then be visible on your construction paper.

If you're using typing paper, use one of the techniques listed above or simply photocopy the pattern. To reduce the "bleed-through" from the back of the page, place black construction paper behind the page you're photocopying. Some patterns may need to be enlarged.

● **Involve the children.** Use the questions provided to draw the children into the stories. If children are familiar with the story you've chosen, have them help tell the story as you cut the figure. Older children will enjoy cutting their own figures along with you as you tell the story. They can even practice the story and tell it to a group of younger children.

So choose your story, grab some scissors and paper, and get started with storytelling magic your kids will love!

OLD TESTAMENT

AND GOD SAID...

PREPARATION

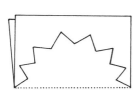

You'll need scissors and construction paper in the following colors: two sheets of yellow and one sheet each of blue, green, brown, red, and orange. Before you begin the story, fold the yellow and red papers in half horizontally. Fold the other colors of paper in half vertically.

THE STORY

Close your eyes and try to imagine... nothing! A long, long time ago, there was... nothing! Nothing to see, nothing to hear, nothing to taste or smell or touch! There was no earth, no world! Now you may open your eyes.

✂ *Begin cutting figure 1 from the yellow paper.*

But God was there. He was thinking and planning and creating. What do you think God was planning? *Let children respond.*

God said, "Let there be light!"

△ *Unfold figure 1.*

What did God call the light? What did God call the darkness? *Let children respond.*

But something was missing.

✂ *Begin cutting figure 2 from the blue paper.*

So God said, "Let there be a space above the water." And a big space came. What did God call the big space? *Let children respond.*

Then God said, "Let the water come together." And SPLASH! What happened? What kind of water did God make? *Let children respond.*

God made rivers and lakes and streams and ponds and oceans.

△ *Unfold figure 2. Hold up the sky and seas as shown.*

So there was sky and there were seas. But something was missing.

✂ *Begin cutting figure 3 from the brown paper.*

God said, "Let's see some dry land." And what happened? What kind of dry land did God make? *Let children respond.*

God made flat deserts, rocky shores, tall mountains, and rolling hills.

△ *Unfold figure 3 and hold the two pieces end to end.*

But something was missing.

✂ *Begin cutting figure 4 from the green paper.*

So God said, "Let plants grow." And up they grew. What kinds of plants

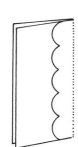

Figure 1

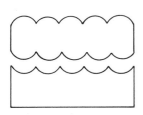

Figure 2

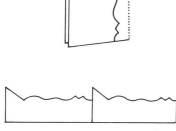

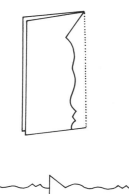

did God make? *Let children respond.*

God made grass, flowers, bushes, vines, and trees.

 *Unfold figure 4.*

But something was missing.

✂ *Begin cutting figure 5 from the yellow paper.*

So God said, "Let lights come in the sky." And lights began to glow. What were those lights? *Let children respond.*

God made the sun for daytime and the moon and stars for nighttime.

 *Unfold figure 5.*

But something was missing.

✂ *Begin cutting figure 6 from the red paper.*

So God said, "Let the waters be filled with swimming creatures. And let the sky be full of flying creatures." God made fish and . . .

 *Unfold figure 6 and let the children discover the birds.*

But something was missing.

✂ *Begin cutting figure 7 from the orange paper.*

So God said, "Let all kinds of animals come onto the land." And they did. What kinds of animals can you think of? What kinds of sounds do those animals make? *Let children respond.*

The animals crawled and jumped and climbed and ran. But there was still something missing. What was it? *Let children respond.*

So God said, "Let's make a person." And God did.

 *Unfold figure 7.*

Then God looked at everything he had made and said, "Everything I've made is very good." What's your favorite thing that God has made?

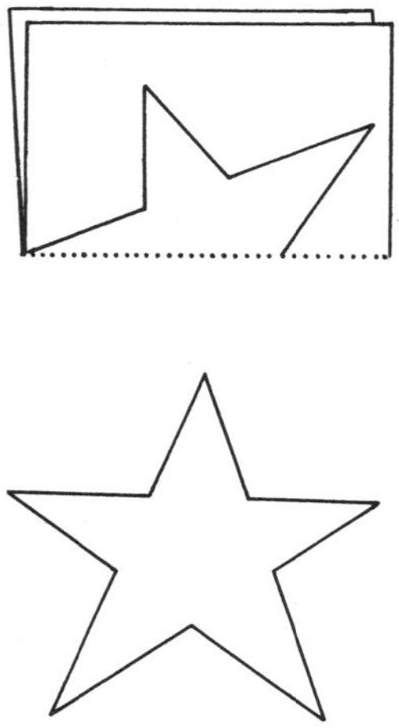

Figure 3

Figure 4

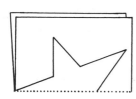

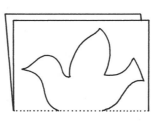

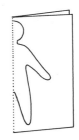

Figure 5

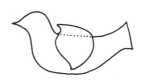

Figure 6

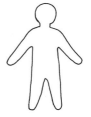

Figure 7

THE FRUIT TREE

PREPARATION

You'll need scissors, one sheet of green construction paper, and one sheet of brown construction paper. Before the story, choose a hiding place large enough to accommodate your whole class.

The patterns for this activity are on pages 13 and 14.

THE STORY

Figure 1

Fold the green paper in half vertically.

When God made the world, he made a man named Adam and a woman named Eve. God let Adam and Eve live in a beautiful, perfect garden.

Cut figure 1 from A to B.

There were all kinds of wonderful things to see *(point to eyes)* and touch *(reach out and touch a child)* and smell *(point to nose)* and hear *(point to ears)*. What could they see? What could they touch? What could they smell? What could they hear? *Let children respond after each question.*

In the garden, there were all kinds of wonderful fruits to taste.

Cut figure 1 from B to C.

Unfold figure 1.

God told Adam and Eve that they could eat the fruit of any tree they wanted, except the fruit from the tree of knowing good and bad. Adam and Eve didn't know bad things. How do we feel when we know bad things? *Let children respond.*

When we know bad things, we feel sad and afraid. God didn't want Adam and Eve to feel sad and afraid. So they weren't allowed to eat fruit from that tree.

Begin cutting the spiral snake (figure 2) from the brown paper. Let the tail dangle down as you cut toward the head.

Adam and Eve enjoyed the wonderful garden they lived in. And everything was fine until, one day, a snake came to Eve.

Finish cutting the snake and hold it up.

The snake said, "Did God say you couldn't eat this fruit from the tree of knowing good and bad?"

Eve said, "Yes."

The snake said, "You really can eat it if you want. Then you'll know good and bad, and you'll be like God." Do you think the snake was telling the

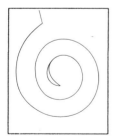

Figure 2

Figure 1

truth? *Let children respond.*

Fold figure 1 again and cut from D to E.

Eve thought about what the snake had told her.

Unfold the figure.

When Eve looked at the pretty fruit, she thought about how wise it would make her. And it looked like it would taste yummy! So she ate some.

Pull the fruit off of the tree.

Then she took the fruit to Adam, and he ate some. After Adam and Eve ate the fruit, a very sad thing happened. Can you guess what that was? *Let children respond.*

Adam and Eve began to know about bad things. They began to feel sad and afraid. They looked for a place to hide. *Lead children to a hiding place you've chosen.*

In the cool part of the day, God came to walk in the garden. But he did not see Adam and Eve. Why not? *Let children respond.*

"Adam and Eve, where are you?" God called.

"We're hiding," Adam and Eve answered.

"Did you eat the fruit I told you not to eat?" asked God.

"Eve gave me some of the fruit," said Adam.

"The snake lied to me and tricked me into eating it," said Eve.

Adam and Eve knew good and bad now. But were they like God? *Let children respond.*

No. They weren't like God. They weren't happy anymore, either.

And because Adam and Eve didn't obey God, they had to leave the wonderful garden.

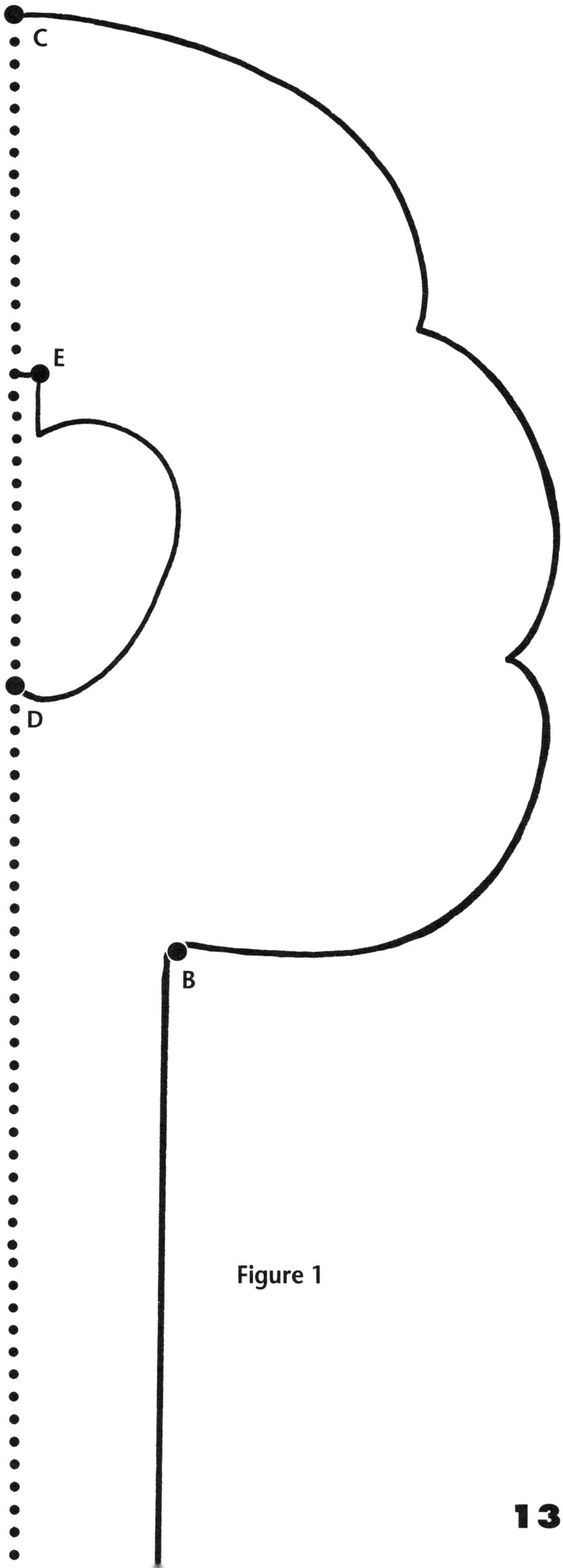

C

E

D

B

Figure 1

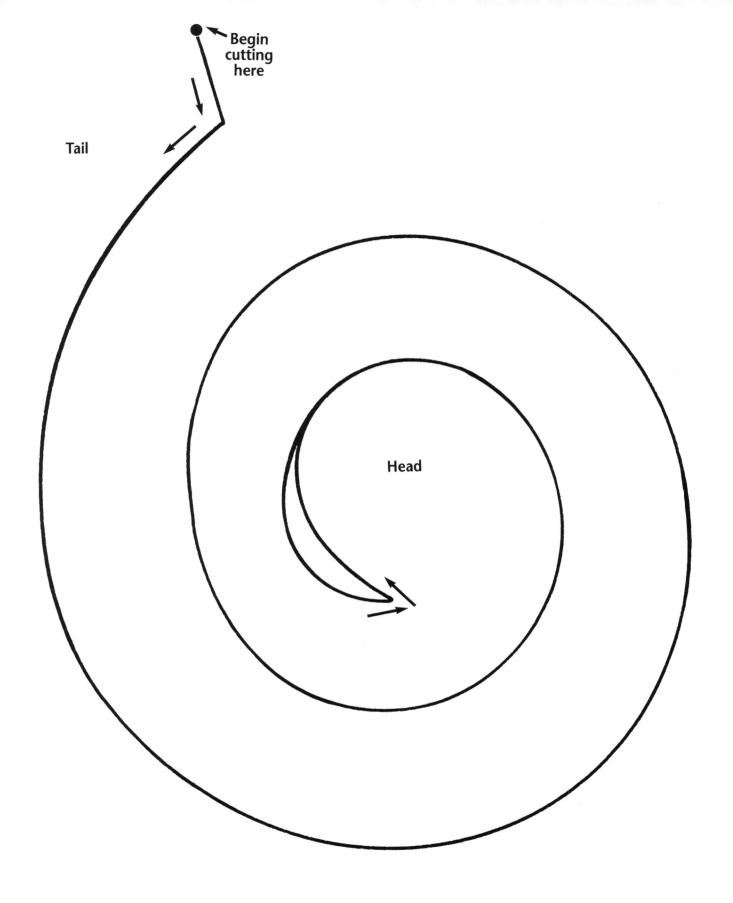

Begin cutting here

Tail

Head

Figure 2

THE BIG HOUSEBOAT

PREPARATION

You'll need scissors and one sheet of brown construction paper. The pattern for this activity is on page 17.

THE STORY

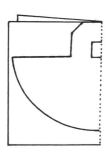

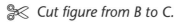 *Fold the paper in half horizontally.*

There was a time, long ago, when people forgot about God. What happens when people forget about God? *Let children respond.*

When people forget about God, they become selfish and mean.

These people had become so mean that God was sorry he made them.

Cut figure from A to B.

But there was one man who still loved God. His family loved God, too. This man's name was Noah.

Cut figure from B to C.

God told Noah to build a big, big boat—big enough to hold Noah's family and many animals. How big do you think that boat would have to be? As big as our room? Bigger than our room? *Let children respond.*

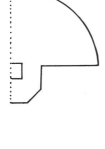

Cut figure from C to D. The figure should now resemble a hammer. Hold it by the "handle" and pretend to hammer.

So Noah got out his tools and followed God's directions. He measured and he sawed and he hammered. *Lead children in "hammering."*

Do you think Noah had any help building that big boat? *Let children respond.*

Noah's family probably helped him.

Cut out section E.

Little by little, they built a huge boat.

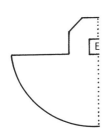

Unfold the figure.

When the boat was ready, God brought two of each kind of animal into the ark. What kinds of animals can you think of? *Let children respond.*

What do you think the ark sounded like with all those animals? *Let children respond.* Let's each think of one kind of animal. When I say go, I want you each to make the noise of the animal you're thinking of. Ready? Go! *Let children make animal noises.*

When all the animals were in the boat, Noah's family went in, and God closed the door. Dark clouds rolled across the sky. There was a great storm. It rained and rained and rained some more. For forty days and forty nights it rained. That's more than a month. What do you think would happen if it rained for more than a month? *Let children respond.*

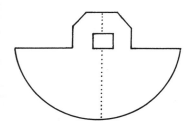

The water got higher and higher, and the big boat began to float. Let's pretend we're in a boat.

☞ *Make the figure dip up and down as if on water. Encourage children to sway back and forth.*

The big boat bobbed up and down on the waves. But everyone in the boat stayed safe and dry.

When the rain stopped, the water slowly went back down, until the boat reached the top of a mountain. There it stayed. How do you think Noah and his family felt when the rain stopped? *Let children respond.*

They came out of the boat, and they thanked God. Then God did a wonderful thing. He painted a rainbow across the sky. The rainbow was a sign of God's promise never to destroy the earth by water again.

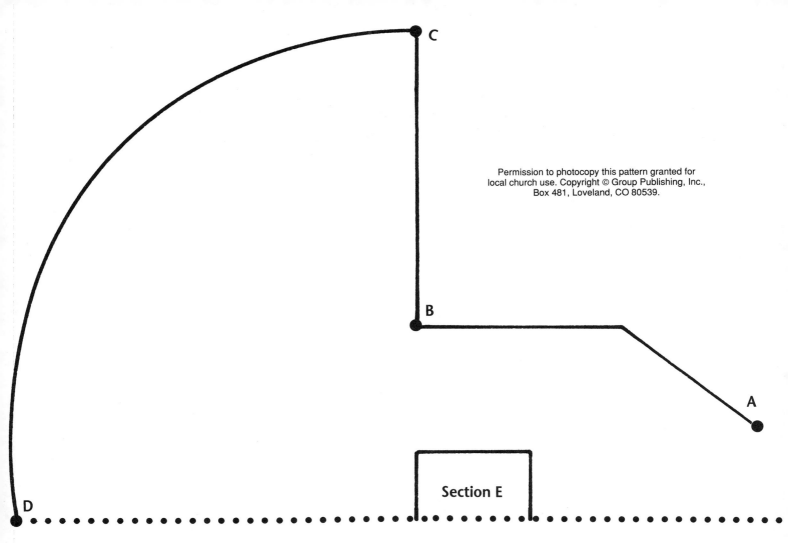

C

B

A

Section E

D

SARAH LAUGHS

You'll need scissors and one sheet of red construction paper.

THE STORY

△ *Fold the paper in half horizontally.*

One day when the sun was shining brightly, a man named Abraham was sitting outside his tent. Have you ever been in a tent? Why do you think Abraham lived in a tent? *Let children respond.*

As Abraham looked across his fields, he saw three men coming.

✂ *Cut along the fold from the edge to F.*

Abraham called to the three men and invited them to eat dinner with him. They said they'd be glad to join Abraham for dinner.

Abraham called to his wife, Sarah, who was in the tent. He told Sarah he was inviting guests for dinner.

✂ *Cut figure from A to B.*

What do you think Sarah did when she heard they'd be having company? *Let children respond.*

Sarah started making dinner right away. While she worked, she listened to the men talking with Abraham.

✂ *Cut figure from B to C.*

While Sarah was listening, the men told Abraham something very special. They told Abraham that he and Sarah would have a baby the next year.

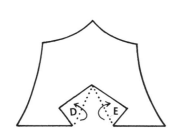

△ *Unfold the figure, and fold out flaps D and E.*

Sarah was surprised. She and Abraham had never had any children, and they were too old now to have a baby. So Sarah laughed when she heard this news.

God said, "Why did Sarah laugh? Is anything too hard for the Lord?" What do you think? Is anything too hard for the Lord? *Let children respond.*

God always keeps his promises. The next year, God's promise came true. Abraham and Sarah *did* have a baby—a baby boy. They named the baby Isaac, which means, "He laughs."

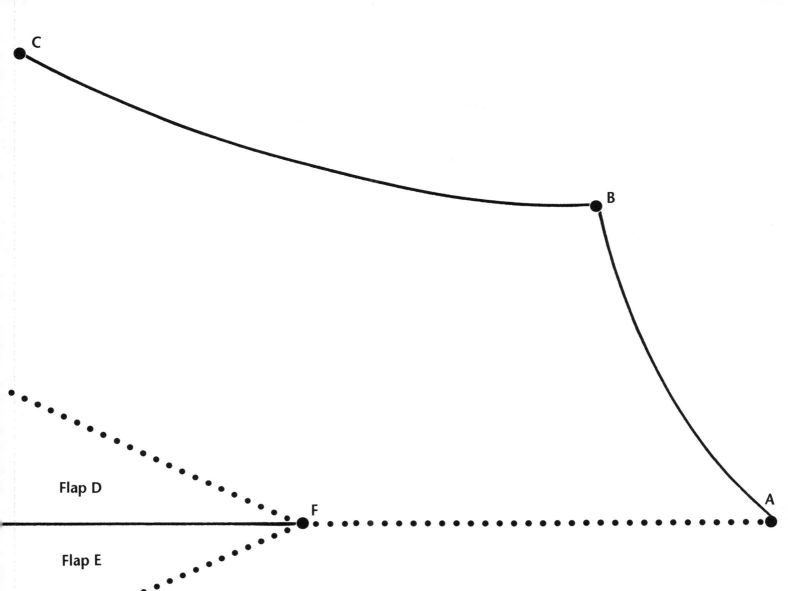

C

B

A

Flap D

F

Flap E

A STAIRWAY TO HEAVEN

PREPARATION

You'll need at least three sheets of construction paper (any color), transparent tape, and a stapler. Before you tell the story, lay the sheets of paper end to end and tape or staple them together.

THE STORY

As you tell the story, fold the paper accordion-style from end to end.

Jacob's brother was mad at Jacob. In fact, he was so mad he wanted to kill Jacob. So Jacob was running away.

Jacob ran a long, long way, out into the countryside all by himself. He kept going all day long. How do you feel after you walk or run a long way? *Let children respond.*

Jacob was very tired. The sun began to go down. But there was no house close by to sleep in. What would you do if you were tired and had no place to sleep? *Let children respond.*

Jacob decided to sleep on the ground. He found a stone to use for a pillow. How would a stone pillow feel? *Let children respond.*

Jacob lay down and went to sleep. During the night, he had a dream. Have you ever had a dream? What was it?

As children respond, attach the top fold of the paper to a wall or bulletin board by taping or stapling. Make sure the paper is attached low enough to reach the floor.

Jacob dreamed that there was a stairway, like a ladder, that went all the way from the earth up into heaven.

Unfold the paper "stairway" and tape the bottom fold to the floor.

Place your hands side by side, with thumbs together and fingers out as shown on page 21. Wiggle your fingers to "fly" your hands like angels up and down the paper stairway. Encourage the children to make angels with their hands, too.

Angels were going up and down this stairway. And God stood at the top. God said, "I will not leave you. I will take care of you wherever you go."

What do you think Jacob thought when he woke up? *Let children respond.*

He said, "Wow! This place is awesome! The Lord is here, and I didn't even know it!" Then Jacob said, "I promise, Lord, that you'll always be my God."

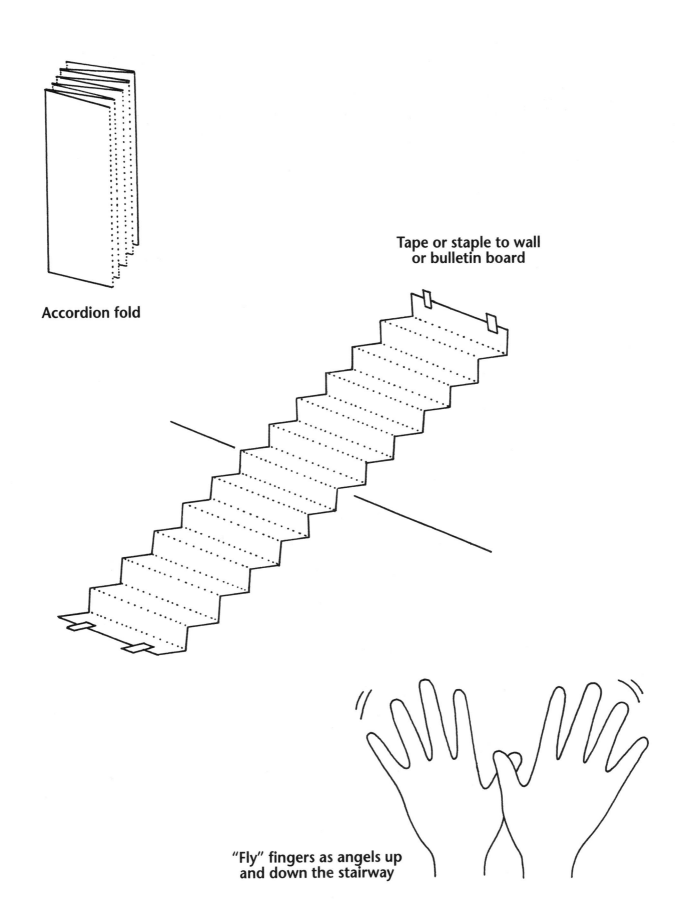

Accordion fold

Tape or staple to wall
or bulletin board

"Fly" fingers as angels up
and down the stairway

A BABY IN A BASKET

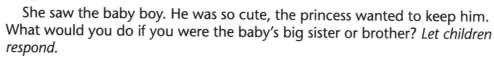

PREPARATION

You'll need scissors and one sheet of typing paper. Before you tell the story, fold one corner of the paper diagonally to meet the opposite side. Cut off and discard the extra paper at the end so you'll have a square.

THE STORY

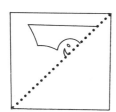

There was once a mean king in Egypt. He didn't like God's people. He hated them so much that he wanted to get rid of all their boy babies. God's people were afraid of this mean king.

✂ *Cut out section A from the folded paper triangle.*

One mother decided to save her baby boy from the king. She carefully made a basket and put her baby in it. Then she put the basket in the river and let it float.

✂ *Cut out section B.*

She trusted God to take care of her baby. And she left the baby's big sister by the river to watch him. Do you have younger brothers or sisters? Do you ever help your parents take care of them? *Let children respond.*

△ *Fold figure on dotted line C and cut out section D.*

While the basket was floating on the river, the king's daughter, the princess, came to the river. She saw the basket and asked her servant to bring it to her. When she looked in the basket, what did she see? *Let children respond.*

△ *Unfold the figure.*

She saw the baby boy. He was so cute, the princess wanted to keep him. What would you do if you were the baby's big sister or brother? *Let children respond.*

The baby's sister ran to the princess. "Would you like me to find someone to care for the baby until he's big enough to go with you?" she asked.

"Yes," said the princess.

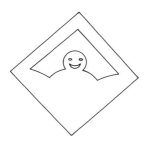

So the baby's sister brought their mother to the princess. The princess gave the baby to his own mother so she could take care of him until he was big enough to live at the palace.

The baby boy grew up to be a great leader of God's people. Can anyone guess what the princess named this baby? *Let children respond.*

The princess named the baby Moses.

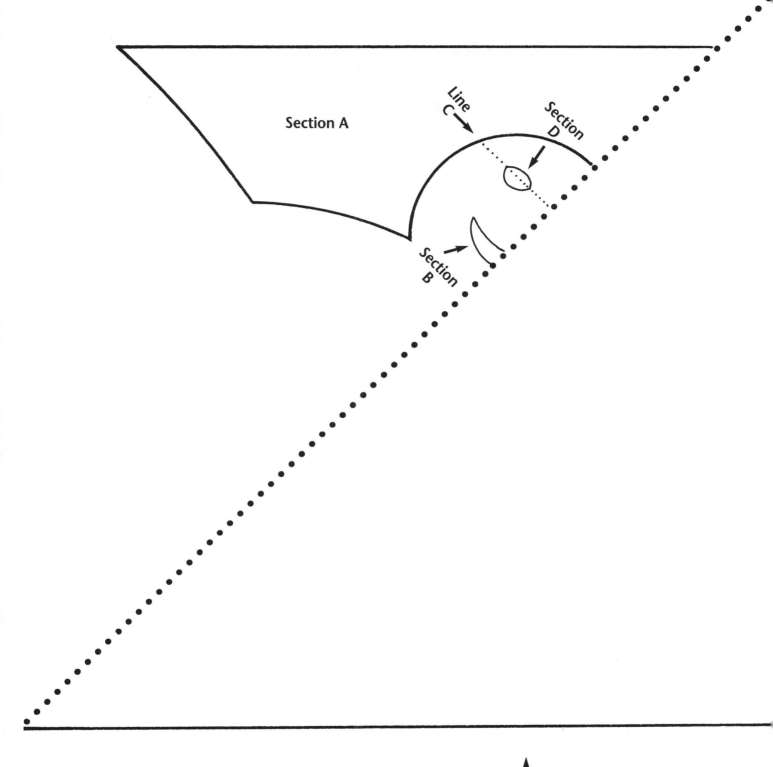

Section A

Line C →

Section D →

← Section B

Cut off and discard this section ↕

A DONKEY WHO TALKED

PREPARATION

You'll need scissors and one sheet of brown or gray construction paper. The pattern for this activity is on page 26.

THE STORY

Fold paper in half vertically.

What's the best thing that's ever happened to you? What's the worst thing? *Let children respond.*

Long ago, the people of Moab said that Balaam was a man who could make good or bad things happen to people. The good things were called blessings, and the bad things were called curses. Whenever Balaam blessed people, good things would happen to them. Whenever Balaam cursed people, bad things would happen to them.

✂ *Cut figure from A to B.*

The king of Moab didn't like God's people. Do you think he wanted to bless them or curse them? *Let children respond.*

The king sent some men to ask Balaam to come and curse God's people. Balaam asked God about it. But God told Balaam not to go. So he didn't.

Line E

✂ *Cut figure from B to C.*

The king sent some more men to Balaam. They told him if he would come and curse God's people, the king would give him a lot of money. Would you like to have a lot of money? *Let children respond.*

Balaam wanted a lot of money, too. The king's offer sounded good to him. So he asked God again if he could go. This time God said he could go as long as he promised to say only what God wanted him to say.

✂ *Cut figure from C to D.*

So Balaam got on his donkey and began to ride to see the king of Moab.

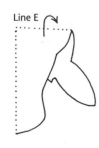

Fold along line E and cut out section F.

As Balaam rode along, God sent an angel to stand in his way. The angel had a sword in his hand. Balaam didn't see the angel.

Unfold the figure.

But Balaam's donkey saw the angel. What would you do if you were a donkey and you saw that angel with a sword? *Let children respond.*

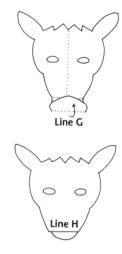

Line G

Line H

Balaam's donkey walked right off the road into a field.

Fold figure up along line G.

Balaam hit his donkey with a stick to make her get back on the road. But as soon as the donkey got back on the road, the angel appeared again.

The donkey moved close to a wall near the road to get away. But this mashed Balaam's foot against the wall. How do you think Balaam felt? *Let children respond.*

Fold figure under along line H.

Balaam beat the donkey again. And she went back to the road. But there was the angel again. This time the donkey sat down right under Balaam. Balaam was so angry that he beat his donkey again.

Then God let the donkey talk.

With one hand, hold the donkey figure in front of your face, like a mask. Put your thumb under the bottom folded section and move it up and down to make the donkey "talk." See the example on page 27.

She said, "What did I do to make you beat me like this?"

Set donkey figure aside.

Do animals usually talk? What would you do if you heard a donkey talk? *Let children respond.*

Balaam answered his donkey. He said, "You made me look like a fool."

Hold donkey figure in front of your face. Move the bottom folded section up and down as the donkey "talks."

The donkey said, "I am your own donkey. Have I ever done this before?"

Set donkey figure aside.

"No," said Balaam.

Then God let Balaam see the angel with the sword. Balaam bowed down. "I know what you are planning to do," said the angel.

What do you think Balaam was planning to do? *Let children respond.*

The angel said, "I came to stop you. Your donkey saved you."

"I'm sorry," said Balaam. "I'll go back home."

"No," said the angel. "Go to the king. But say only what God tells you to say."

What do you think Balaam did? *Let children respond.*

Balaam went to see the king. But when it was time for Balaam to curse God's people, he blessed them instead.

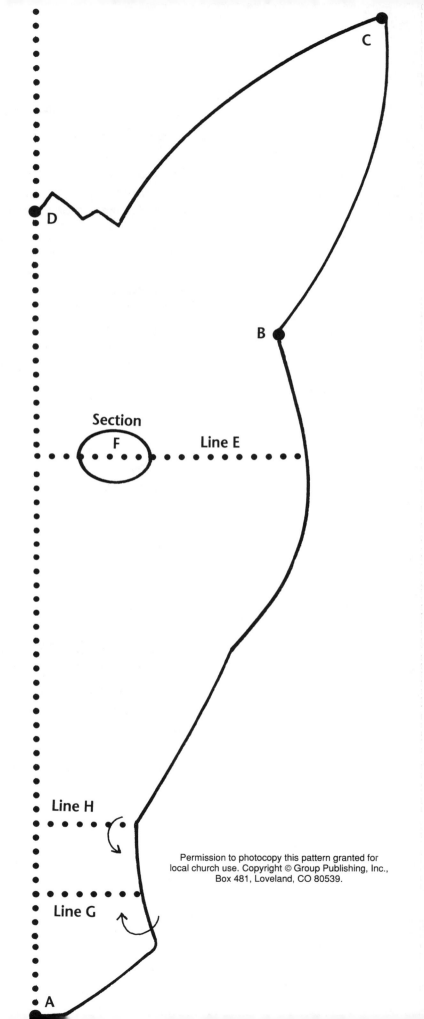

C

D

B

Section
F

Line E

Line H

Line G

A

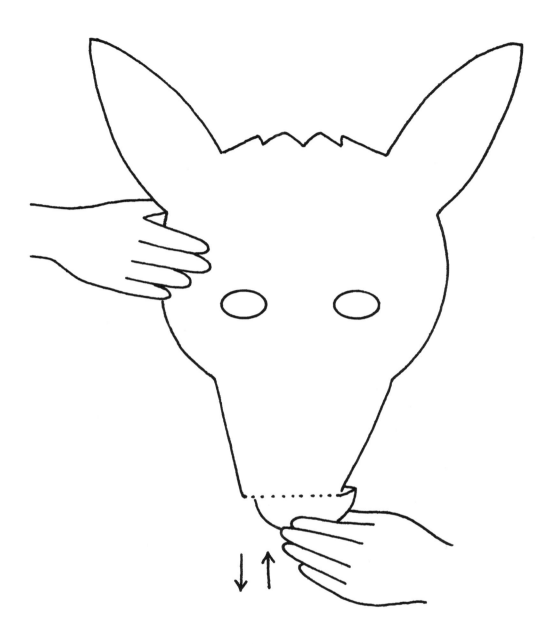

**Move the bottom folded section up and
down to make donkey "talk"**

THE WALLS THAT FELL

You'll need scissors and one sheet of typing paper.

THE STORY

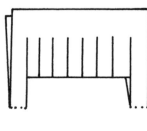
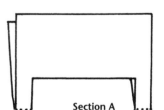
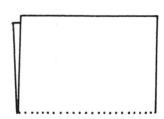
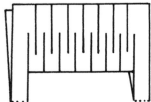

Section A

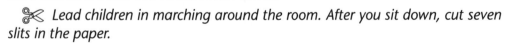 *Fold the paper in half horizontally.*

Joshua was the leader of God's people long ago. God told Joshua to lead his people to a new land where they would live. And Joshua did.

Cut out section A and discard it.

But there was a problem. When Joshua got to that new land, there were some enemies living there. These enemies were people who didn't love God or obey him. Some of them lived in a city called Jericho. The city of Jericho had a big wall around it.

Begin cutting eight slits in the paper.

Joshua didn't know how to get through the walls of Jericho. But he trusted God. And God had a plan. He told Joshua how to capture Jericho without even fighting. He told Joshua and the people to march around the city walls one time every day for six days. So they did.

Then the next day, God told them to march around the city seven times. Let's march around our room seven times.

Lead children in marching around the room. After you sit down, cut seven slits in the paper.

Ask the children to help you count as you cut, "One, two, three, four, five, six, seven."

After they had marched around seven times, the leaders blew their trumpets, the people gave a loud shout, and the walls just fell down.

Unfold the paper and shake it out. Let the children step through the hole that has been made in the paper "wall."

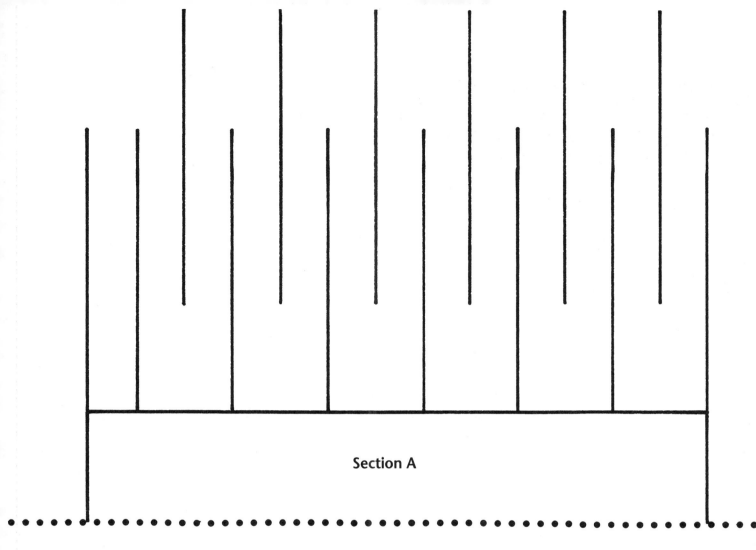

Section A

THE DAY THE SUN STOOD STILL

PREPARATION

You'll need scissors and one sheet of yellow construction paper.

THE STORY

Fold the paper in half horizontally.

Joshua led God's people into the land God promised to give them. God's people did a lot of fighting to capture the promised land. How would you feel if you heard that people from far away were trying to take over our country? *Let children respond.*

The people who lived in the land of Gibeon were afraid of God's people. So they made peace with God's people. Joshua didn't attack them.

Begin cutting out the figure at point A.

Now the kings of the other nearby countries heard that the men from Gibeon were on God's side. So these kings gathered their armies together and went to fight the men from Gibeon. What would you do if you were from Gibeon? *Let children respond.*

The men from Gibeon sent a message to Joshua. "Help! Come quickly!" the message said. So Joshua marched his army to Gibeon to help. God told Joshua, "Don't be afraid. I'll help you win."

Joshua's men marched all night to get to Gibeon. They surprised the kings from the other countries. They fought with those kings all day. God even threw large hailstones down from the sky onto the enemies. But Joshua knew God's people would need extra daylight to win the fight that day. What do you think might happen if the sun went down before the fight was finished? *Let children respond.*

So Joshua said, "Sun, stand still. Moon, stand still."

Unfold the figure.

And the sun stopped right where it was. It didn't move across the sky. It didn't go down for another whole day. The Bible tells us that God had never done that before. God was fighting for his people that day.

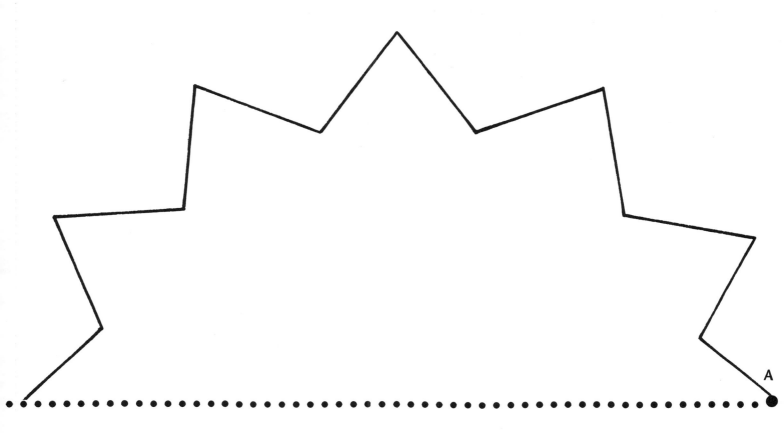

A

SAMSON

You'll need scissors, one sheet of yellow or orange construction paper, two sheets of typing paper, transparent tape, and a marker.

THE STORY

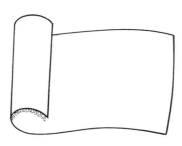

👉 *Roll the yellow paper into a tube and tape it.*

Samson was a leader of God's people. God told Samson never to cut his hair. And as long as Samson obeyed God, he was the strongest man around. Why do you think Samson was so strong? Was it because his hair was long or because he obeyed God? *Let children respond.*

✂ *Begin cutting slits in the tube.*

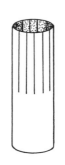

Samson had a girlfriend named Delilah. Samson also had some enemies. They wanted to catch Samson, but they couldn't, because he was too strong for them. They asked Delilah to find out what made Samson so strong. She said she would try. What would you do if some enemies wanted you to find out a secret about a friend? *Let children respond.*

👉 *As you tell the next few paragraphs, bend down the strips that you've cut.*

So Delilah asked Samson, "What makes you so strong?"

Samson said, "If you tie me with seven new bow strings, I won't be strong." Was Sampson telling the truth? Do you think he knew he couldn't trust Delilah? *Let children respond.*

That night, Delilah tied him with the bow strings. Then she called the enemies to catch him. Can you guess what Samson did? *Let children respond.*

When the enemies tried to catch Samson, he snapped the bow strings off and fought them away.

Each time Delilah asked Samson how he got so strong, Samson made up a different answer. And each time the enemies came, Samson escaped.

👉 *Tear off a few strips on one side of the cylinder and draw a face.*

Delilah asked Samson one last time, "What makes you so strong?"

Finally Samson told Delilah, "If you cut my hair, I won't be strong anymore." Why do you think Samson finally told the truth? What do you think happened next? *Let children respond.*

While Samson was asleep, Delilah called a man to cut his hair.

✂ *Snip off the strips of "hair."*

And then Samson wasn't strong anymore. Why do you think he lost his strength? Was it because his hair was short or because he disobeyed God? *Let children respond.*

When the enemies came this time, they caught him and put him in their jail.

☞ *Roll one piece of the typing paper and tape it into a cylinder.*

A little while later, some of the enemies had a big party. They brought Samson to the party so they could make fun of him. Samson stood by some big posts that held up the roof of the building. He prayed, "Lord, remember me. Make me strong one more time, so I can win over the enemies."

☞ *Roll and tape the other piece of the typing paper. Stand the two cylinders on end to represent pillars.*

God did make Samson strong. Samson pushed down the posts that held the building up, and the house crashed down on all the enemies.

☞ *Push the paper pillars down.*

RUTH'S KINDNESS

PREPARATION

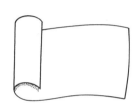

You'll need scissors, one sheet of yellow construction paper, transparent tape, and a pencil.

THE STORY

Has your family ever moved from one house to another? *Let children respond.*

There was once an old woman named Naomi. She was going to move to a different land all by herself. But there was a young woman in her family named Ruth. Ruth said, "I'll go with you. Then you won't be all alone." So Ruth and Naomi moved to Bethlehem.

👉 *Roll the paper and tape it into a tube.*

Ruth and Naomi didn't have jobs to make money to buy food. How could they get food to eat? *Let children respond.*

Ruth had an idea.

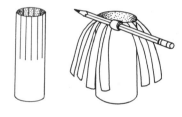

✂ *Begin cutting slits in the top of the tube as shown.*

Ruth said, "Let me go into the field where the farmer's men are cutting down the grain. I'll pick up some of the leftover grain."

👉 *Using the pencil, roll some of the strips under. Pull the pencil out gently, making curving strips around the tube.*

So Ruth went to the grain fields. She picked up the grain that the workers left behind. What do you think she did with the grain? Do you think Naomi was glad that Ruth had moved with her? *Let children respond.*

The farmer saw Ruth picking up the leftover grain. He told his workers to drop some of the grain on purpose. Why do you think he did that? *Let children respond.*

The farmer wanted to give Ruth more good grain to pick up.

👉 *Tear off some of the strips and drop them.*

The workers did what the farmer told them to do. They dropped extra grain for Ruth to gather and take home.

Ruth was kind to work hard to help Naomi. And the farmer was kind to leave extra grain for Ruth to take home. Can you think of things you can do to be kind to people? *Let children respond.*

34

SAUL BECOMES A KING

PREPARATION

You'll need scissors and one sheet of yellow construction paper. The pattern for this activity is on page 36.

THE STORY

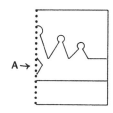

△ Fold the paper in half horizontally.

God's people wanted a king. Why do you think they wanted a king? *Let children respond.*

They wanted to be like other countries around them. They went to God's prophet Samuel and said, "Ask God to give us a king." So God chose a king for his people. He was a young man named Saul.

✄ Cut out and discard section A.

Samuel told Saul he would soon be the king of God's people. Saul was surprised when he heard this news. He didn't tell anyone what Samuel had said. Why did he keep it a secret? *Let children respond.*

✄ Cut figure from B to C.

Saul was a very shy man. When it was time for Saul to become the king, no one could find him. They looked and looked.

✄ Cut figure from C to D.

Samuel asked God, "Is Saul here yet?"

God said, "Yes, he is hiding behind the boxes and bags."

Some of the people ran to look behind the boxes and bags, and there they found Saul. They brought him out. He stood taller than anyone else.

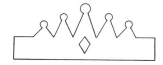

✄ Cut figure from D to E.

Samuel said, "This is the man God has chosen to be your king."

△ Unfold the figure.

All the people shouted, "Long live the king!"

35

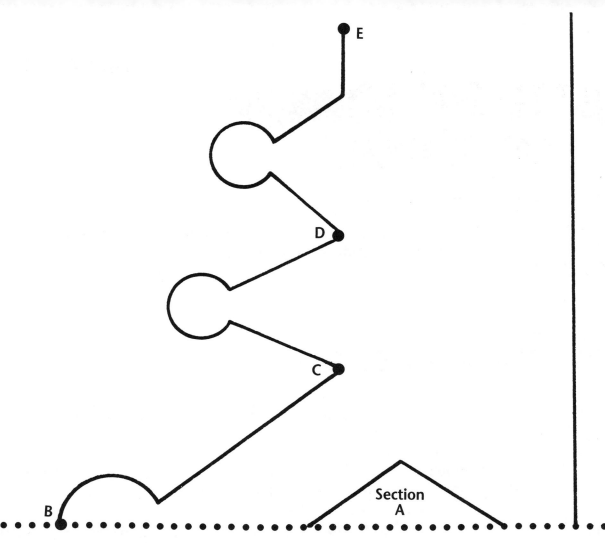

E

D

C

B

Section
A

DAVID AND THE GIANT

PREPARATION

You'll need scissors and one sheet of construction paper. The pattern for this activity is on page 39.

THE STORY

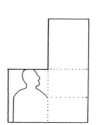

There was once a mean giant named Goliath. Goliath did not love God. And he didn't love God's people. In fact, Goliath went with the enemy army to fight God's people.

✂ *Cut out and discard section A.*

✂ *Cut figure from B to C.*

First, Goliath tried to scare God's people. How do you think he did that? *Let children respond.*

Goliath yelled, "Send a man to fight me. If he wins, we will be your servants. But if I win, you will all be our servants."

◣ *Fold the tall side of the paper down at line H, then up at line J. Fold back at line K so the pattern is on top.*

God's people were scared. No one wanted to fight Goliath. Why were they so scared? *Let children respond.*

They were scared because they didn't know what to do.

✂ *Cut figure from D to E.*

Then David, a shepherd boy, stepped up. "I'll fight Goliath," he said. Everyone laughed to think of a shepherd boy fighting a giant.

✂ *Cut figure from E to F.*

But David didn't think it was funny at all. He went to a stream and picked up five smooth stones. He put them in his pouch. Then he walked out to meet the giant.

✂ *Cut figure from F to G, then unfold.*

Now the giant laughed. "I'll feed you to the birds," he said to David. How would you feel if a giant said that to you? *Let children respond.*

But David said, "You come to me with a shield and a sword, but I come to you in the name of the Lord."

Then David put one of the stones into his sling, and he swung the sling around and shot the stone out. The stone flew through the air. It hit Goliath

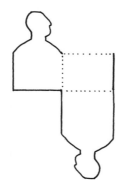

right in his forehead. And Goliath crashed to the ground and never got up again.

△ *Fold the giant figure down.*

How could such a little boy win against a big giant? Who helped David fight Goliath? *Let children respond.*

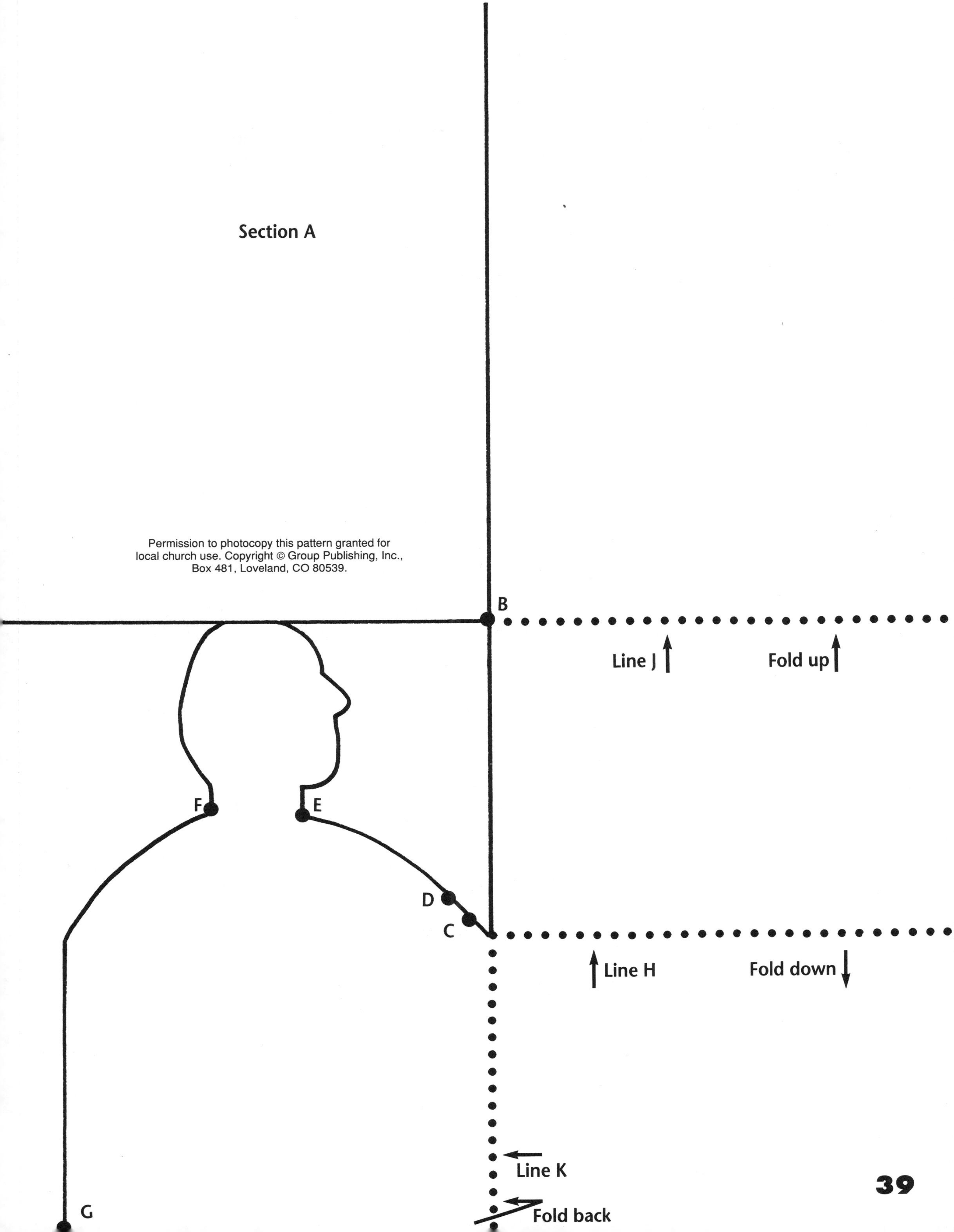

Section A

B

Line J ↑   Fold up ↑

F   E

D

C

↑ Line H   Fold down ↓

← Line K

← Fold back

G

39

BIRDS FEED ELIJAH

PREPARATION

You'll need scissors and one sheet of black construction paper.

THE STORY

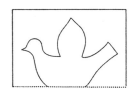

Fold the paper in half horizontally.

Elijah was a man of God. God gave Elijah messages to take to mean King Ahab. Ahab didn't like Elijah's messages, and he didn't like Elijah.

✂ *Cut figure from A to B.*

One time, God sent Elijah to King Ahab with bad news for King Ahab's country. Elijah told the message to the king. "Because you're so mean, God won't send any more rain, not even any dew on the ground, for many years." What happens when it doesn't rain for a long time? *Let children respond.*

✂ *Cut figure from B to C.*

No plants grew, and the people had no food. The king's people got hungry. The king got hungry. Even Elijah got hungry.

✂ *Cut figure from C to D.*

But God was taking care of Elijah. He showed Elijah where to find a little stream. Why did Elijah need a little stream? *Let children respond.*

Elijah could drink water from the stream.

Fold wings down.

But God did more to help Elijah. God sent raven birds to Elijah every morning and every night.

Holding the figure on its belly, move it up and down to make the wings flap as if flying.

Each time the ravens came, they brought bread and meat to Elijah. That's the way God took care of Elijah. How does God take care of you? *Let children respond.*

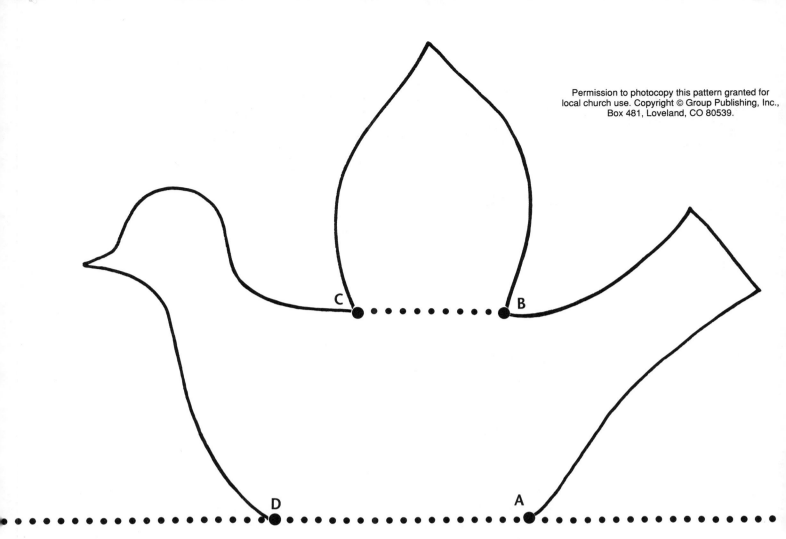

SHARING A LITTLE OIL AND FLOUR

PREPARATION

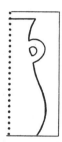

You'll need scissors and one sheet of construction paper.

THE STORY

△ *Fold the paper in half vertically.*

Elijah, the man of God, had been living by a stream. Elijah drank water from the stream, and God sent birds with food for Elijah. But day after day came and went, and still there was no rain.

What do you think happened to the stream? *Let children respond.*

The stream dried up. Elijah knew he couldn't stay there, but he didn't know where to go. So God told Elijah, "Go to a town in Sidon. You can stay there. I have told a woman who lives there to give you food."

✂ *Cut figure from A to B.*

Elijah obeyed God. He went to Sidon. He saw a woman gathering sticks at the town gate, so he said, "Would you bring me some water and bread?"

✂ *Cut figure from B to C.*

The woman said, "I have only enough oil and flour to make one more supper for myself and my son. Then I'll be out of food."

What do you think the woman should do? Why? *Let children respond.*

✂ *Cut figure from C to D.*

Elijah said, "Don't be afraid. Go ahead and make me some bread. And make some for yourself and your son. God won't let you run out of oil or flour."

✂ *Cut figure from D to E.*

Do you think she believed Elijah? *Let children respond.*

The woman went home and made bread for her family and for Elijah. They all ate.

✂ *Cut out section F.*

△ *Unfold the figure.*

And when it was time for the next meal, there was still oil and flour to make bread. The oil and flour didn't run out, just as God had promised. And Elijah and the woman and her family had enough to eat.

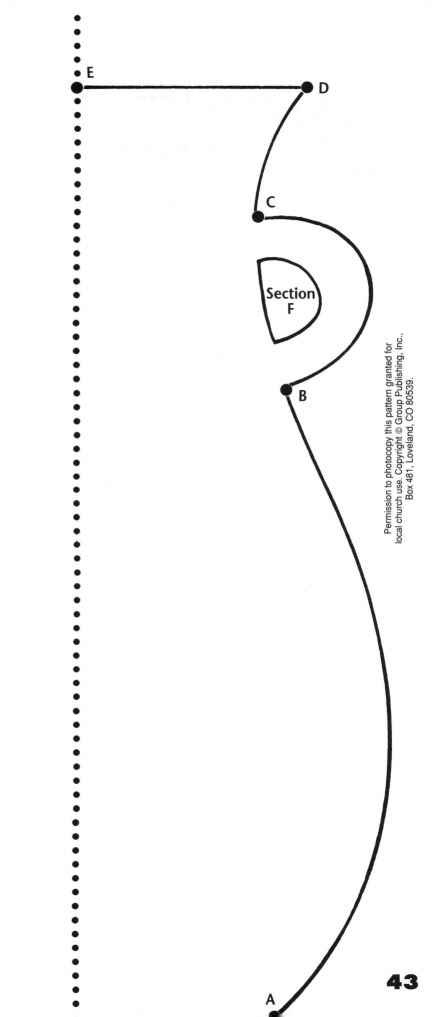

E ●————————————● D

C

Section
F

B

A

ELIJAH AND THE ALTAR OF FLAMES

PREPARATION

You'll need scissors, one sheet of brown construction paper, one sheet of orange construction paper, and transparent tape.

THE STORY

Mean King Ahab didn't believe in God. He worshiped a stone idol named Baal.

✂ *Cut orange paper in half lengthwise.*

Elijah, the man of God, called all the people of the country to come to a mountain. He said, "If Baal is God, then we should worship him. But if the Lord is God, then we should worship him. Let's find out which one is the true God."

How do you think they could do that? *Let children respond.*

"We'll build worship altars," said Elijah.

✂ *Cut the brown paper in half lengthwise.*

"Then we'll ask Baal to send fire to his worship altar and ask the Lord to send fire to his worship altar. The one who sends fire will be the true God."

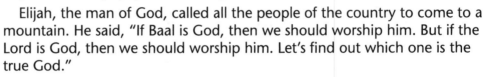

☞ *Tape the end of one orange paper to the end of one brown paper. Set aside extra orange and brown paper for another use.*

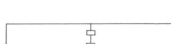

So the people who worshiped Baal stacked stones together to make a worship altar for Baal.

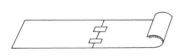

☞ *Begin slowly and loosely rolling up the paper from the orange end.*

Elijah stacked stones together to make a worship altar for the Lord. The people of Baal began to pray to Baal to ask him to send fire to their altar.

They prayed and prayed, but no fire came. Why not? *Let children respond.*

"Pray louder," said Elijah. "Maybe his mind is on something else." Do you think that's why Baal didn't answer? *Let children respond.*

"Or maybe he's busy," said Elijah. Do you think that's why he didn't answer? *Let children respond.*

"Or maybe he's on a long trip," said Elijah. Do you think that's why he didn't answer? *Let children respond.*

"He might even be asleep," said Elijah. Do you think Baal was asleep? Is that why he didn't answer? *Let children respond.*

 *Tape the roll of paper into a tube to represent the altar.*

The people of Baal cried louder and louder. But no fire came. Why not? *Let children respond.*

Then Elijah dug a ditch around the altar he had built for the Lord. He told men to pour water all over the altar. They poured so much water on it that the altar overflowed and the ditch filled up with water.

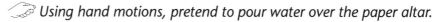 *Using hand motions, pretend to pour water over the paper altar.*

Elijah prayed, "Oh Lord, show us that you are God." What do you think happened? *Let children respond.*

Reach into the paper altar and gently pull out the orange paper part of the way.

Snip around the orange paper with scissors and curve it outward to represent fire.

Fire came and burned up the stones, the ground, and even the water in the ditch. All the people said, "The Lord is God! The Lord is God!"

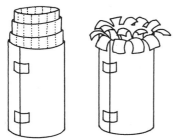

MORE AND MORE JARS OF OIL

PREPARATION

You'll need scissors, transparent tape, and three sheets of typing paper. Copy the pattern onto one sheet. Before you begin, tape the sheets of paper together end to end.

The pattern for this activity is on page 48.

THE STORY

There was once a very sad woman.

△ *Begin folding the paper accordion-style, making folds at least 4 inches wide. Make sure the pattern is on top.*

This woman's husband had died. Now she was in trouble, because her husband owed money to another man. The other man came to see the woman after her husband died. He said, "Pay me the money your husband owed me."

The woman didn't have enough money to pay the man. So the man said he'd take her sons to work for him. The woman was upset. She went to see Elisha, the man of God.

✂ *Cut figure from A to B and from B to C.*

"How can I pay back this man?" she asked. "I don't want him to take my sons away to work."

✂ *Cut figure from D to E.*

What do you think she could do? *Let children respond.*

"Do you have anything at your house that you can sell to make money?" asked Elisha.

✂ *Cut figure from E to F and from F to G.*

"I have nothing at home," she said. "Just a little bit of oil."

✂ *Cut figure from G to H.*

"Get jars from your neighbors and friends," said Elisha. "Pour your oil into the jars and then sell the oil."

✂ *Cut figure from H to I.*

What do you think the woman thought about this idea? What do you think? Will the idea work? *Let children respond.*

The woman went home. Her sons went to their neighbors and friends and got empty jars. They brought them to their mother, and she began pouring oil from her jar into the other jars.

✂ *Cut figure from J to K and from K to L. Cut out handles.*

And the oil didn't run out. She poured and poured and poured. She filled all the jars.

◺ *Unfold the figure and spread out the jars.*

Then they took the jars and sold them. They made enough money to pay back the man all her husband owed him.

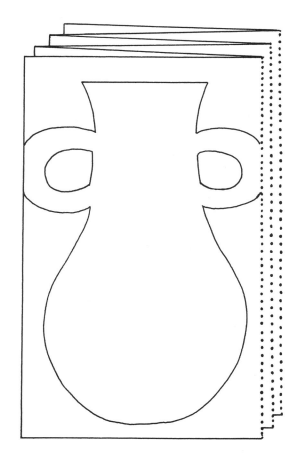

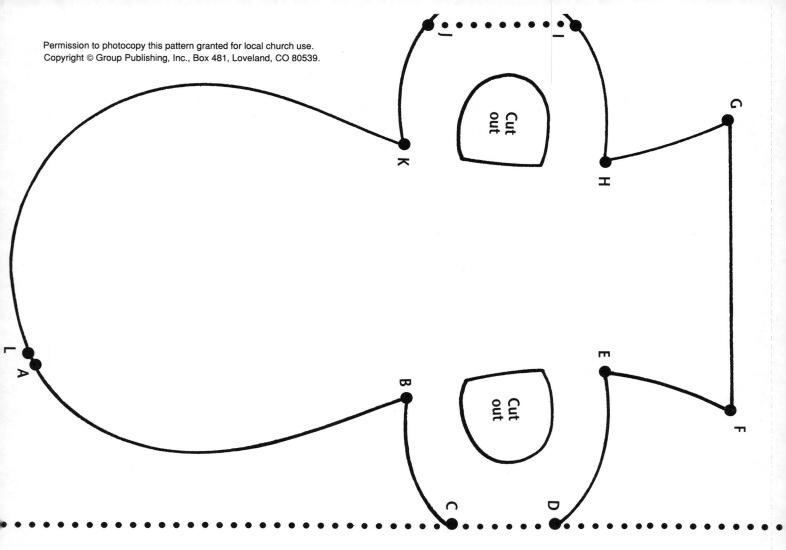

Cut out

Cut out

THE HANDWRITING ON THE WALL

PREPARATION

You'll need scissors and one sheet of typing paper.
The pattern for this activity is on page 51.

THE STORY

⊿ *Fold the paper in half vertically.*

King Belshazzar lived in the land of Babylon, far away from the land where God's people lived. King Belshazzar didn't believe in God. In fact, his country had fought with God's people. Men from his country had taken gold cups from God's temple. And they had taken young men away to serve them. One of these young men was Daniel.

What do you know about Daniel? *Let children respond.*

Daniel loved God, and God loved Daniel. God made Daniel very wise. Daniel could figure out hard problems. One night, King Belshazzar had a party.

✂ *Cut figure from A to B.*

The king and his friends drank out of the gold cups that belonged in God's temple. Suddenly, a hand appeared and started writing something on the wall.

✂ *Cut figure from B to C.*

All the king's friends were scared. How would you have felt if you saw that hand? *Let children respond.*

The king's knees began to shake. He tried to read the writing. It said, "Mene, mene, tekel, parsin." King Belshazzar couldn't understand that language. Can you? *Let children respond.*

✂ *Cut figure from C to D.*

The king called for all of his wise men to come and tell him what the writing meant. But his wise men didn't understand it. Then someone said, "Daniel will know. Call Daniel."

✂ *Cut figure from D to E.*

So the king called for Daniel. When Daniel came, he said, "I'll tell you what this means."

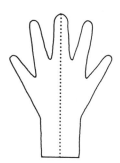

⊿ *Unfold the figure.*

"God sent this hand to write on the wall to send you a message because you worship idols of stone and wood and metal instead of worshiping God. The writing says that God isn't going to let you be king anymore."

And that very night, an enemy army came in and took over King Belshazzar's kingdom.

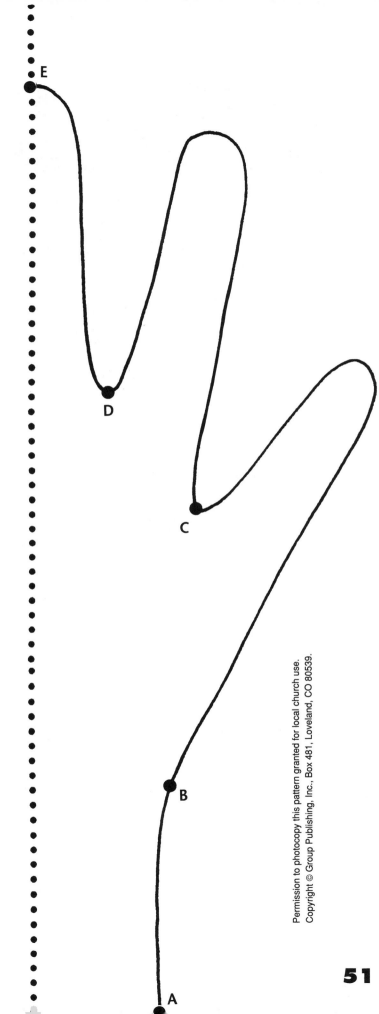

E

D

C

B

A

DANIEL IN THE LIONS' DEN

PREPARATION

You'll need scissors and one sheet of gold or brown construction paper. Before you tell the story, fold one corner of the paper diagonally to meet the opposite side. Cut off and discard the extra paper at the end. Unfold the paper into a square.

The pattern for this activity is on page 54.

THE STORY

Daniel was one of the leaders of the country of Persia. He loved and obeyed God. Three times every day, he went upstairs to his room and knelt down by his window to pray to God.

Can you think of some times when you pray? Where can you pray? *Let children respond.*

Fold the paper in half, matching side C to side A.

God blessed Daniel. Daniel was such a good, wise, honest worker that the king decided to put Daniel in charge of the whole kingdom.

Fold side D toward side B. Crease on the fold line.

When the other leaders found out, they were jealous. Why were they jealous? *Let children respond.*

They didn't want Daniel to be in charge of them. They tried to find something about Daniel they could complain about to the king, but they couldn't find anything wrong with Daniel.

Cut out section E.

Unfold side B.

Finally, they figured out a way to trap Daniel. They went to the king and said, "Why don't you make a new law? Anyone who prays to any god except you, O King, will be thrown into the lions' den."

Cut lines F and G.

Unfold the figure completely.

This sounded good to the king, so he made it a law. What do you think the other leaders did then? *Let children respond.*

When Daniel found out about the law, he just went home and prayed. He asked God for help.

Begin folding the figure as if making a snowflake.

As you continue the story, fold corner H to corner I, then J to K, then J–K

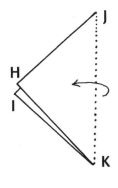

to H–I.

But the other leaders were watching for Daniel to pray. They caught him praying and told the king about it. The king was sorry, because he liked Daniel very much. But the king could not change the law. Once something was a law, it had to stay a law. So they threw Daniel into the lions' den.

✂ *Cut a zig-zag pattern across the end of the figure.*

△ *Unfold the figure and push section F forward.*

What do you think the king did after they threw Daniel into the lions' den? *Let children respond.*

The king worried. He didn't eat or sleep at all that night. When the sky began to get light the next morning, he hurried to the lions' den. He called, "Daniel, was your God able to save you?"

👉 *Pull the bottom of the mouth forward as shown. Crease the lower mouth, then open.*

👉 *Repeat with the top of the mouth.*

"Yes," answered Daniel. "God sent his angel to close the lions' mouths."

The king was very happy. He let Daniel out of the lions' den. The king said, "Daniel's God is the real God. He has saved Daniel from the lions."

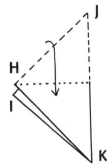

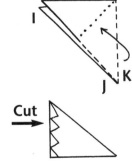

Cut

Pull out lower lip and crease as you fold the figure.

Pull out upper lip and crease as you fold the figure.

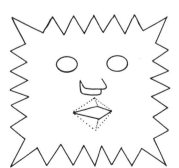

53

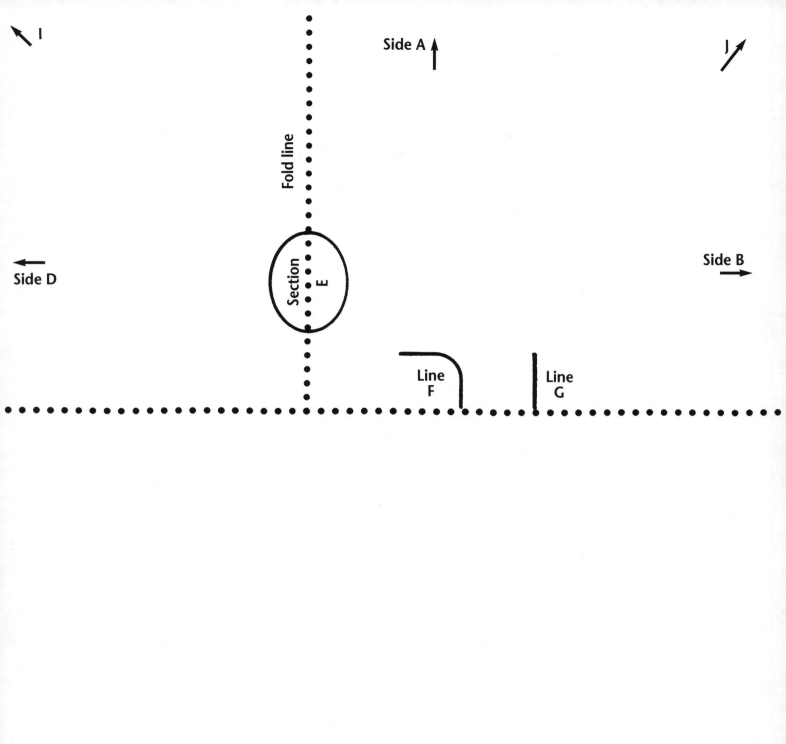

I

Side A ↑

J

Fold line

Side D ←

Section E

Side B →

Line F

Line G

K

Side C ↓

H

Cut off and discard ↓

JONAH AND THE WHALE

PREPARATION

You'll need scissors and one sheet of typing paper.
The pattern for this activity is on page 57.

THE STORY

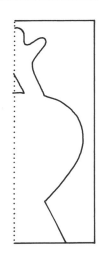

△ *Fold the paper in half vertically.*

One day God spoke to a man named Jonah. God said, "I want you to go to a city called Ninevah. Ninevah is a city full of people who do bad things. I want you to tell them to start doing what's right."

But Jonah didn't want to go. Was there ever a time when you didn't want to do what you were told to do? What did you do? *Let children respond.*

Jonah decided to run away from God. He went to a city by the sea and got on a ship that was sailing far away.

✂ *Cut figure from A to B.*

But God knew what Jonah was doing. He sent a strong wind and a powerful storm. The waves beat against the ship. How do you think the sailors on that ship felt? *Let children respond.*

The sailors were afraid the ship would break apart. They started throwing their boxes and baggage into the sea to make the ship lighter.

✂ *Cut figure from B to C.*

The captain came to Jonah. "Why has this terrible storm come?" he said. "Pray to your God. Maybe he will help us!"

✂ *Cut figure from C to D.*

Jonah said, "I know why this storm has come. It's because I'm running away from God."

✂ *Cut figure from D to E.*

"What can we do?" asked the sailors.

✂ *Cut figure from E to F.*

"You can throw me into the sea," said Jonah.

✂ *Cut out section G.*

△ *Unfold Jonah figure, hold vertically, and mark eyes on Jonah.*

☞ *Display Jonah and keep the whale figure horizontal so kids don't focus on*

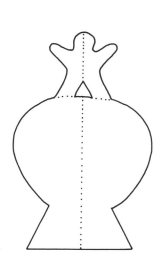

55

it as you tell the next section of the story.

The sailors didn't want to throw Jonah into the sea. They tried to row the ship to the shore, but they couldn't. The storm only got worse. Finally, they threw Jonah into the sea. Right away the storm stopped. The ship and the sailors were safe.

As for Jonah, God sent a huge fish to swallow him.

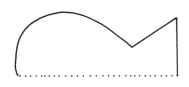 *Fold the Jonah figure down at his feet and fold the fish figure closed again.*

Hold the figure horizontally to show the fish (with Jonah inside).

What do you think it was like in the belly of a huge fish? *Let children respond.*

While Jonah was inside the fish, he prayed. "I called to you, Lord. The waves came over me, but you saved me. I'll do what you asked me to do."

Then God told the fish to spit Jonah out, and it did. Jonah was on dry land again.

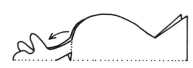 *Still holding the fish horizontally, pull the Jonah figure out to show the fish spitting him out.*

God said again, "Go to the city called Ninevah and tell the people what I told you to say before."

And this time, Jonah did!

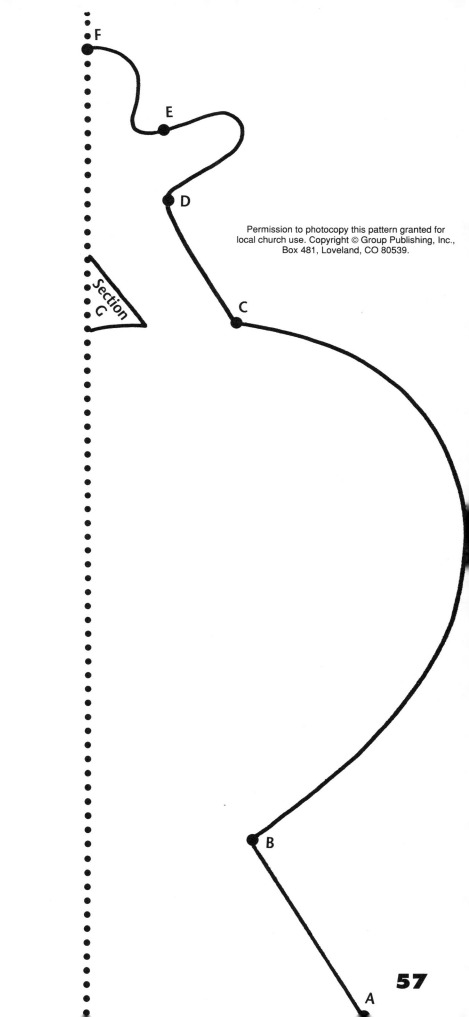

F

E

D

C

Section G

B

A

57

NEW TESTAMENT

JESUS IS BORN

PREPARATION

You'll need scissors and one sheet of typing paper.
The pattern for this activity is on page 63.

THE STORY

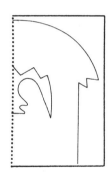

△ *Fold the paper in half horizontally.*

✂ *Begin cutting figure from A to B.*

The town of Bethlehem was very busy. People had come from many different places to be in Bethlehem. Everyone who was born in Bethlehem had come back to be counted. The king wanted everyone to be counted so he would know how many people were in his kingdom.

✂ *Cut figure from B to C.*

A man named Joseph came to Bethlehem to be counted. He brought his wife, Mary, with him. Mary was going to have a baby soon. Does anybody remember how Mary found out she would have a baby? *Let children respond.*

God sent an angel to Mary. The angel told Mary that her baby would be God's son. The angel also brought this news to Joseph and told Joseph to name the baby "Jesus."

✂ *Cut figure from D to E.*

When Joseph and Mary got to Bethlehem, they started looking for a place to spend the night. They looked and looked and looked, but all the rooms were full because of all the people who had come to Bethlehem to be counted. Have you ever had to look for a place to spend the night when you've been on a trip with your family? What would you do if you couldn't find a room? *Let children respond.*

Mary and Joseph looked for a long time. Finally, they found somewhere they could sleep. The only empty room in the whole city of Bethlehem was a stable where the animals stayed. So that's where Joseph and Mary stayed, too. How would you feel if you had to stay in a stable with animals? How would you stay warm? What would you use for a pillow? *Let children respond.*

✂ *Cut figure from E to F.*

While Mary and Joseph were staying in the stable, the baby was born.

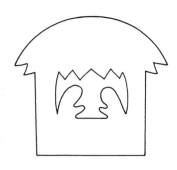

Who was this baby? Why was he special? *Let children respond.*

This baby was God's son, Jesus. Mary carefully wrapped the baby in soft cloth and laid him in a manger.

✂ *Cut figure from F to G.*

◿ *Unfold the figure.*

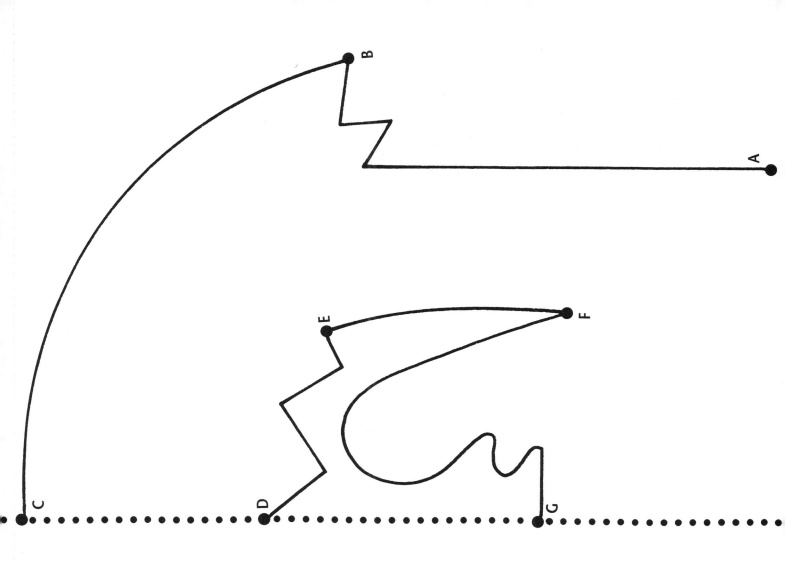

A

B

C

D

E

F

G

THE SHEPHERDS IN THE FIELD

You'll need scissors, transparent tape, and several sheets of typing paper. Copy the pattern onto one sheet. Before you begin, tape the sheets of paper together, end to end.

THE STORY

As you tell the first paragraph, fold the paper accordion-style into an equal number of panels. Make sure the pattern is on top.

It was night. Out in the fields near Bethlehem, some sheep were resting. Shepherds were taking care of them. The night was very dark and quiet, until suddenly an angel appeared to the shepherds. The shepherds were very scared. How would you feel if you saw an angel? *Let children respond.*

The sheep must have wondered what was happening, too, because the darkness suddenly turned to light, and the glory of the Lord shone all around.

Cut figure from A to B.

The angel said, "Don't be afraid. I'm bringing you good news of great joy. Today in Bethlehem a savior, God's son, has been born. He is Christ Jesus, the Lord. You'll find him in a manger."

Cut figure from C to D.

Suddenly a whole choir of angels came to stand by the first angel.

Unfold the figures.

They said, "Glory to God in the highest! Let there be peace on earth!" Let's all say that together like the angels did. "Glory to God in the highest! Let there be peace on earth!" Why were all the angels singing? Why was Jesus' birth so important? *Let children respond.*

After the angels went back to heaven, the shepherds said, "Let's go to Bethlehem. Let's see for ourselves this thing that has happened."

When the shepherds got to Bethlehem, they found baby Jesus in a manger, just as the angel had told them. The shepherds went back to their sheep, praising God for what they'd seen and heard.

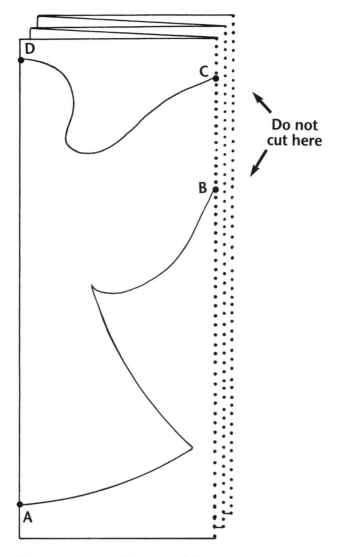

D

C

Do not
cut here

B

A

**You may copy this actual figure
on your paper as a pattern**

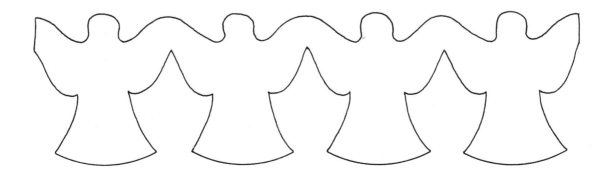

THE STAR

PREPARATION

You'll need scissors and one sheet of yellow construction paper.

THE STORY

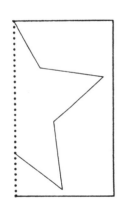

Long ago, there lived some wise men. They liked to study and find out about things. They especially liked to learn about the sky and the stars. What do you like to learn about? *Let children respond.*

One night these wise men saw a special star. They thought it might be a sign. They studied the star and decided it was a sign that a king had been born.

They decided to go and see the new king. After they packed gifts for the king, they set out on their journey. How do you think they knew which way to go? How did they travel? *Let children respond.*

 *Fold the paper horizontally.*

The wise men went over long roads.

✂ *Cut figure from A to B.*

They went up steep mountains.

✂ *Cut figure from B to C.*

They went down hills.

✂ *Cut figure from C to D.*

They went across a flat desert.

✂ *Cut figure from D to E.*

They went on curvy roads and straight roads.

✂ *Cut figure from E to F.*

 *Unfold the figure and hold it high.*

All this while, the wise men were following the star. And pretty soon, the star led them right to the baby king. They gave him their gifts. They bowed down and worshiped him.

Who was this baby king? *Let children respond.*

This baby king was Jesus, God's own son.

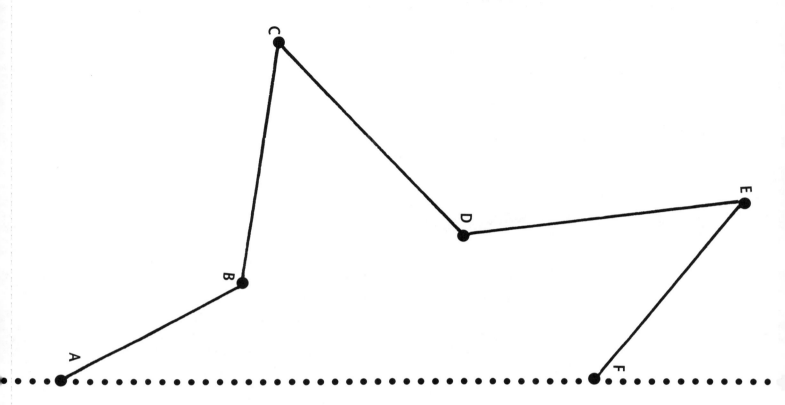

THE WISE MEN

You'll need scissors and one large sheet of construction paper. As you tell the story, you'll be folding the paper into six panels. Mark off the places where you'll fold the paper.

The pattern for this activity is on page 70.

THE STORY

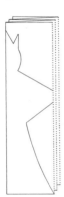

△ *As you tell the first paragraph, fold the paper into six panels, accordion-style. Make sure the pattern is on top.*

Wise men from the East saw the special star that God put in the sky as a sign that a new king had been born. These wise men packed gifts and traveled days and nights to get to Jerusalem so they could see this king. They went to the old king, Herod, and asked him where they could find the new king.

✂ *Cut figure from A to B.*

Herod was surprised. He didn't know about any new baby king. How do you think Herod felt when he heard there was another king in his kingdom? *Let children respond.*

King Herod asked his friends if they knew where to find the baby king. Herod's friends told him that, long ago, God had said a king was supposed to be born in Bethlehem.

✂ *Cut figure from B to C.*

King Herod sent the wise men to Bethlehem. He said, "When you find this baby king, tell me. I want to come see him, too." Do you think Herod was telling the truth? Did he really want to see the baby king? *Let children respond.*

Herod didn't like the baby king. He wanted to be the only king in the kingdom. Herod wanted the wise men to help him find the baby king so he could get rid of him.

✂ *Cut figure from D to E.*

The wise men went on to Bethlehem. They watched the special star. It led them right to the baby king.

✂ *Cut figure from E to F.*

How do you think the wise men felt when they finally found the baby Jesus? How would you feel if you were one of those wise men? *Let children respond.*

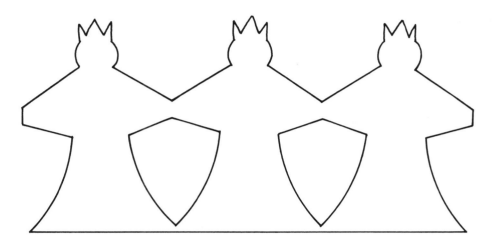 *Unfold the figure.*

The wise men were very happy. They bowed down and worshiped baby Jesus. They gave him presents of gold and incense and myrrh. What kind of present would you give to the baby Jesus? *Let children respond.*

That night, an angel warned the wise men in their dreams not to help Herod find the baby. They went back home a different way, and the baby Jesus was safe.

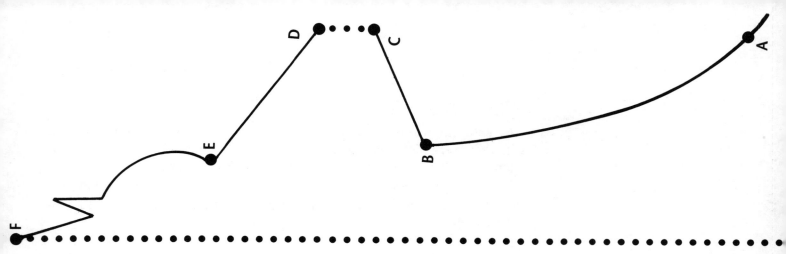

ZECHARIAH AND THE ANGEL

PREPARATION

You'll need scissors and one sheet of typing paper.
The pattern for this activity is on page 73.

THE STORY

Fold the paper in half horizontally.

Zechariah was an old man who worked at the temple. His wife was named Elizabeth. They didn't have any children.

One day, Zechariah was working in the temple. Many people were outside praying. They were waiting for Zechariah to come out and lead them in worship.

✂ *Cut figure from A to B.*

But while Zechariah was inside, an angel came to him. Zechariah had never seen an angel before, and he was scared.

Fold figure in half again.

But the angel said, "Don't be afraid, Zechariah. God has sent me to tell you that you and Elizabeth will have a baby. The baby will be a boy, and you should name him John. He will be a great man of God."

✂ *Cut figure along line C.*

This news was hard for Zechariah to believe. "How do I know you're telling me the truth?" he asked.

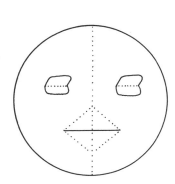

"You don't believe me," said the angel. "You won't be able to talk until what I've said comes true." Would you believe a message you heard from an angel? *Let children respond.*

Unfold the figure.

Fold up figure's eyelids.

The people outside were still waiting for Zechariah. What do you think they thought when Zechariah took so long? *Let children respond.*

When Zechariah finally came out, he couldn't talk. He could only motion with his hands. How do you think Zechariah felt when he tried to talk, but no words came out? What do you think the people thought then? *Let children respond.*

The people knew Zechariah had seen something amazing.

71

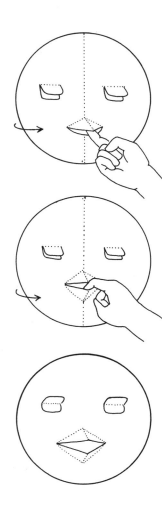

Fold figure again and cut along line D.

The angel's promise came true. Zechariah and Elizabeth did have a baby. When the day came to name the baby, neighbors and family came. It was a very special day. But Zechariah still couldn't talk. So everyone decided to name the baby Zechariah, after his father.

Open figure slightly, and with index finger, push section E inside and crease it.

Elizabeth said, "We'll name him John."

But everyone else said, "He should be named after someone in your family. And no one in your family is named John." Finally they asked Zechariah what he wanted to name the baby.

Open figure slightly, and with index finger, push section F inside and crease it.

Zechariah took out a writing tablet and wrote, "His name is John."

Right away, Zechariah was able to talk again. Why was Zechariah able to talk again? How do you think his friends and family felt when they heard him speak after all that time? *Let children respond.*

Unfold the figure.

The folds you just made will form a mouth that will open and close as you gently pull and push on the sides of the figure's head.

Zechariah began to praise God. His friends and family were amazed.

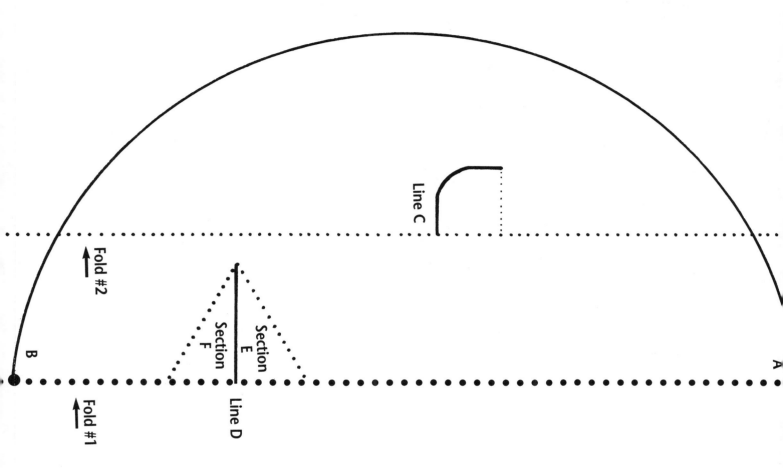

Line C

Fold #2

B

Fold #1

Section F

Section E

Line D

A

JESUS' FRIENDS

You'll need scissors, transparent tape, a pencil, and four sheets of typing paper or a sheet of butcher paper about 44 inches long. If you're using typing paper, copy the pattern onto one sheet. Lay the sheets of typing paper end to end and tape them together. As you tell the story, you'll be folding the paper accordion-style into 24 panels. Mark off the places where you'll fold the paper with a pencil.

THE STORY

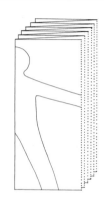

▱ *Begin folding the paper as you tell the first paragraph. Make sure the pattern is on top.*

Jesus went many places to tell people about God. He healed sick people. He cheered up sad people. He helped many people understand what God was really like.

✂ *Cut figure from A to B.*

People from everywhere came to hear Jesus talk and to be healed and blessed by him. Jesus decided to choose some special helpers to help him teach and heal people.

✂ *Cut figure from C to D and from E to F.*

Jesus asked these special helpers to come with him to the hill country.

▱ *Unfold the figures one by one as you call their names.*

First he chose Peter and his brother Andrew. Then he chose James and John. Jesus called James and John "the Sons of Thunder." Why do you think they were called that? *Let children respond.*

Peter, Andrew, James, and John were all fishermen. They left their boats and their fishing nets to follow Jesus.

Jesus also chose Philip and Philip's friend, Bartholomew. Then he chose Matthew. Matthew was a tax collector. What does a tax collector do? *Let children respond.*

Jesus needed a few more helpers. He chose Thomas and another man named James. Do you think it was confusing to have two helpers named James? How could Jesus tell them apart? *Let children respond.*

Jesus also chose Thaddaeus, Simon, and Judas. Jesus let Judas be in charge of the money bag.

These friends traveled with Jesus and helped him. How can you be a friend of Jesus? How can you help him? *Let children respond.*

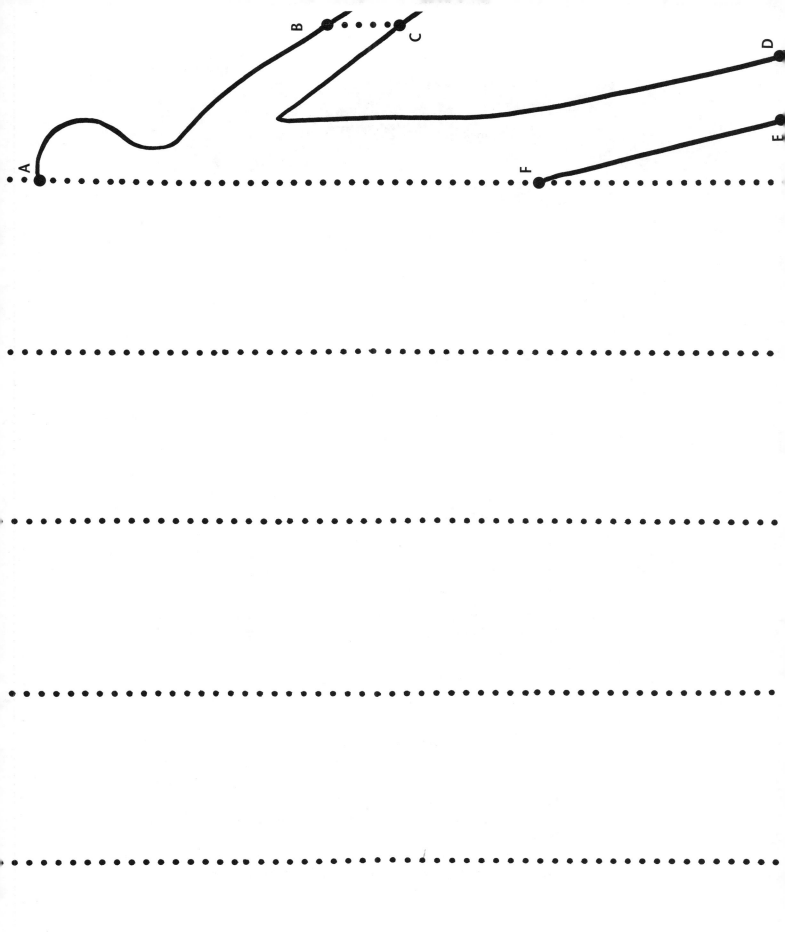

THE MAN WHO CAME THROUGH THE ROOF

You'll need scissors, a marker, and one sheet of typing paper.

THE STORY

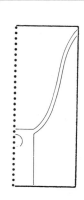

Fold the paper in half vertically.

One day, four men came to Jesus. They were carrying a sick friend on a mat.

Cut figure from A to B.

Their friend couldn't walk. They were hoping Jesus would heal him. Why did they think Jesus might heal their friend? *Let children respond.*

Cut figure from C to D.

When they got to the house where Jesus was, they had a problem. The house was so crowded with people that they couldn't get in. What could they do to get into that house? *Let children respond.*

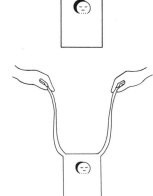

Cut figure along line E.

They thought and thought. Finally they had an idea. They carried their friend up to the roof of the house, and they made a hole in the roof.

Unfold the figure.

Fold the figure's head up and draw eyes and a mouth.

They lowered their friend down on his mat through the hole in the roof, right in front of Jesus.

Holding the figure by the long strips, lower the figure to the floor.

What do you think the people around Jesus thought when they saw a man coming through the roof? What do you think Jesus thought? *Let children respond.*

When Jesus saw the sick man, he said, "Stand up. Pick up your mat. You can walk home now."

The man's legs began to work again. He stood up, picked up his mat, and walked home! The people in the house with Jesus were amazed. Everyone praised God.

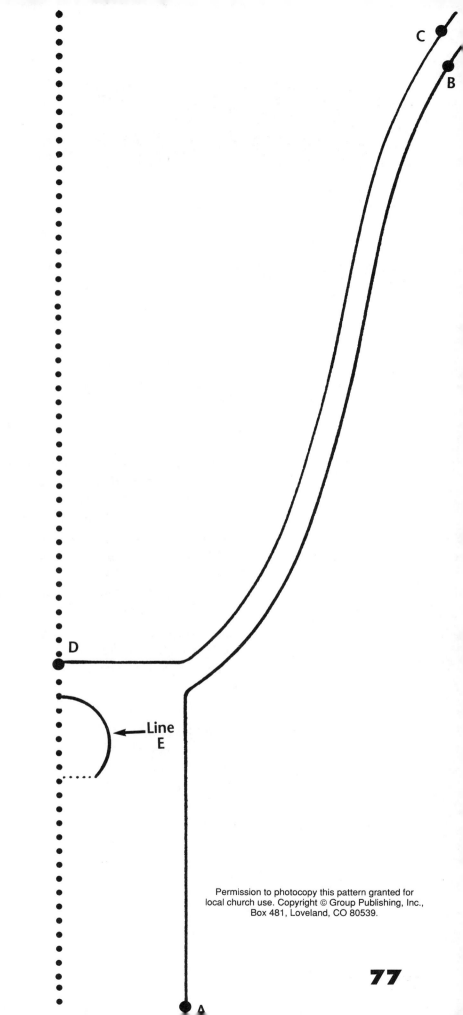

C

B

D

Line
E

A

THE LILIES OF THE FIELD

PREPARATION

You'll need scissors, transparent tape, one sheet of white paper, one sheet of yellow or pink paper, and a pencil. Place the colored paper on top of the white paper and roll both sheets together into a cone shape. Tape the cone to secure it and trim away the pointed top.

THE STORY

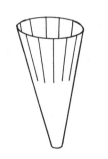

✂ *As you tell the first paragraph, cut half-inch strips from the wide end toward the narrow end of the cone.*

Jesus sat on a mountainside teaching many people. As Jesus taught, he saw birds flying in the air, sitting on tree branches, or just hopping on the grass, singing their bird songs.

Jesus said, "Look at the birds. They don't plant seeds. They don't grow their own food. But God gives them the food they need. So don't worry about getting enough food to eat. God will take care of you." What are some things we worry about? *Let children respond.*

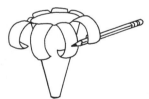

☞ *Roll each strip down around a pencil. Slide the pencil out carefully so the strips stay curved downward.*

Jesus also said, "Look at the flowers in the field." What kinds of flowers do you know? What colors are flowers? *Let children respond.*

"Flowers don't make their own clothes," said Jesus. "God gives them clothes that are more beautiful than kings' or queens'."

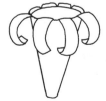

☞ *Show the finished flower.*

Then Jesus said, "God knows you need food to eat and clothes to wear, so you don't need to worry. If God takes care of the birds and flowers, he'll take care of you, too."

What other ways does God take care of you? *Let children respond.*

Zacchaeus & The S

Luke 19:1-10

Vs 4: "Sycamore tree"

This was a "sycamore Fi
Some call it a "mulbe
(Looks like a mulberry
but the Fruit resembl
- An easy tree to climb

camore Tree

" tree.
y" tree.
tree w/ its leaves,
es a Fig).
often planted by the roadside.

THE SOWER AND THE SEEDS

PREPARATION

You'll need scissors and one sheet of green construction paper. Fold the paper accordion-style. Make the top and bottom panels about 3 inches wide. Make the rest of the panels about 1 inch wide. Make sure the pattern is on top. Using another sheet of paper, cut out "seeds." Have the "seeds" ready to drop during the story.

The pattern for this activity is on page 81.

THE STORY

Once Jesus told a story about a farmer who was planting seeds. Have you ever planted seeds? How did you take care of your seeds after you planted them? *Let children respond.*

In Jesus' story, some of the farmer's seeds fell on the hard pathway.

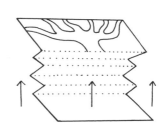

👉 *Drop a paper seed on the floor.*

Could the seeds grow on the hard pathway? *Let children respond.*

✂ *Cut figure from B to C.*

The birds found those seeds and ate them up. The seeds that fell on the hard pathway are like God's word that can't grow in a hard heart.

✂ *Cut figure from D to E.*

Some of the seeds fell on stony ground.

👉 *Drop another paper seed.*

The roots of those seeds couldn't go down very far. When the seeds grew into plants, the plants had tiny, thin roots. Guess what happened when the hot sun shone down on those plants? *Let children respond.*

✂ *Cut figure from F to G.*

The sun dried up those tiny plants. The seeds that fell on the stony soil are like people who only trust God when life is going well. When problems come, those kind of people stop trusting God. What do you do when you have a problem? *Let children respond.*

✂ *Cut figure from H to I.*

Some of the seeds fell among the weeds.

👉 *Drop another paper seed.*

Can you guess what happened to the seeds that fell in the weeds? *Let children respond.*

The weeds were growing fast, and soon they choked out the new little plants that came from those seeds.

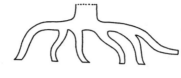

✂ *Cut figure from J to K.*

The seeds that fell among the weeds are like people who let their worries about life choke out their trust in God.

But other seeds fell into the good ground.

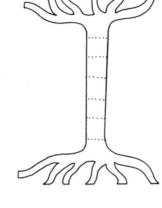

☞ *Drop the rest of the paper seeds.*

What do you think happened this time? *Let children respond.* The roots of these seeds went down deep.

☞ *Show the folded figure with the "roots" pointed down.*

So the plant grew and grew.

◺ *Unfold the figure.*

☞ *Holding the figure with the "roots" pointed down, pull up gradually to make the figure "grow."*

The seeds that fell on the good ground are like people who believe in God and keep on loving God. Every day they grow more and more loving, like Jesus.

What kind of soil are you like? What can you do to grow more like Jesus? *Let children respond.*

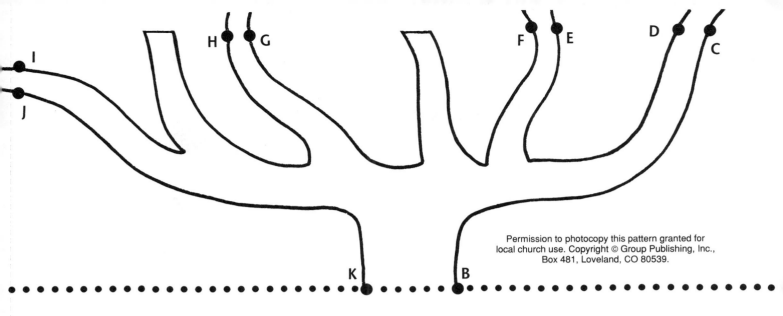

WIND AND WAVES

PREPARATION

You'll need transparent tape, scissors, one sheet of light blue construction paper, one sheet of dark blue construction paper, and a 3-inch square piece of brown construction paper. Before telling the story, cut the two sheets of blue paper in half vertically, using a scalloped line.

Alternating light and dark blue pieces, tape the blue paper end to end.

THE STORY

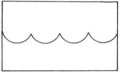

Have you ever sailed in a boat? *Let children respond.*

Jesus and his friends sailed across a big lake one day.

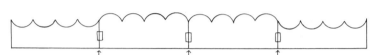 *Fold the brown paper in half horizontally and cut out a semicircle to make a boat. Do not unfold.*

Jesus was very tired, so he lay down in the back of the boat and fell asleep. While he was sleeping, a big storm blew across the lake.

 *Roll the blue paper into a loose cylinder and tape it.*

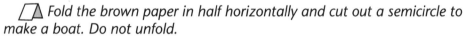 *Carefully pull up the center of the blue paper up to show waves.*

Waves pounded against the boat. Wind blew it this way and that.

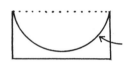 *Set the boat on the waves.*

How would you feel if you were in that boat in the storm? *Let children respond.*

Jesus' friends were scared. "Help, Jesus!" they cried. "Don't you care if we all sink?"

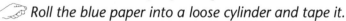 Do you think Jesus cared? *Let children respond.*

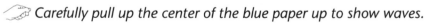 Jesus got up. He talked to the wind and the waves. "Peace! Be still!" he said.

The wind suddenly became quiet. The waves suddenly became still.

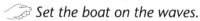 *Push the blue paper back down into the cylinder shape.*

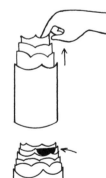 Jesus' friends could hardly believe it. "Even the wind and waves obey Jesus," they said.

 How can you obey Jesus? *Let children respond.*

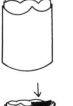

JESUS FEEDS 5,000 PEOPLE

You'll need transparent tape, scissors, and four sheets of typing paper. Copy the pattern onto one sheet. Before you begin the story, tape the sheets of typing paper together end to end.

The pattern for this activity is on page 85.

THE STORY

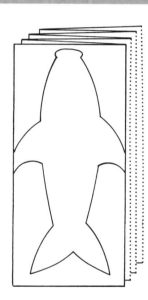

As you tell the first paragraph, fold the paper accordion-style into panels. Make sure the pattern is on top.

Jesus was teaching outside one day. There were 5,000 people standing and sitting around him, listening to him. Jesus saw that it would soon be dinner time. What happens to people when it gets close to dinner time? *Let children respond.*

Jesus knew the people would be getting hungry. "We need to get these people something to eat," Jesus said.

Cut figure from A to B.

How much do you think it would cost to buy food for 5,000 people? Do you think Jesus and his friends had enough money to buy all that food? *Let children respond.*

"We don't have enough money to buy food for all these people," said Philip.

Cut figure from C to D.

Andrew said, "Here's a little boy who has brought five loaves of bread and two fish with him. But that's not enough food for all these people."

Cut figure from D to E.

How many loaves and fish do you think it would take to feed 5,000 people? *Let children respond.*

But the boy gave his loaves and fish to Jesus. Jesus told all the people to sit down. Then he thanked God and began handing the bread and fish to the people.

Cut figure from E to F.

Jesus' friends helped Jesus pass out the food.

Unfold the figure and show many fish.

They didn't run out of bread and fish until all the people had been fed. And when all the people were finished, Jesus' friends picked up twelve baskets of leftovers.

Jesus fed 5,000 people with only five loaves and two fish!

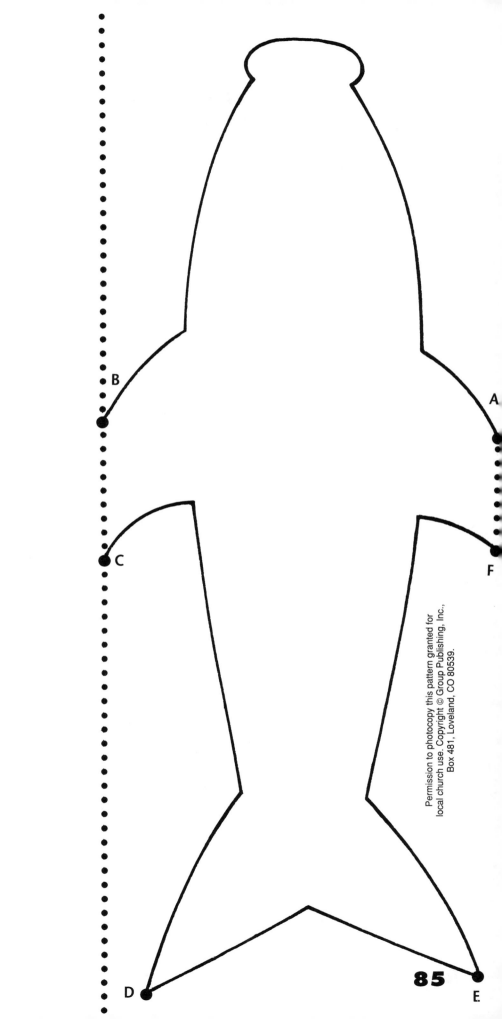

B

A

C

F

85

D

E

BLIND BARTIMAEUS

You'll need scissors and one sheet of typing paper.

THE STORY

△ *Fold the paper in half vertically, and then in half vertically again.*

There was once a man named Bartimaeus. Bartimaeus was blind. Have you ever met a blind person? Let's cover our eyes for a minute and see what it would be like to be blind. *Let children respond.*

Bartimaeus sat by the side of the road close to the city of Jericho. Bartimaeus sat by the road and begged people to give him money. Why did he need money? *Let children respond.*

✂ *Cut figure along line A.*

One day, Bartimaeus heard that Jesus was leaving Jericho and would be passing right by him. Bartimaeus began to call out, "Jesus, be kind to me! Jesus, be kind to me!"

△ *Unfold figure halfway.*

Some of the people said, "Shhhh! Be quiet, Bartimaeus!" Why do you think they wanted Bartimaeus to be quiet? *Let children respond.*

Bartimaeus called louder. "Jesus, be kind to me! Jesus, be kind to me!"

✂ *Cut out section B.*

Jesus heard Bartimaeus and asked the people to bring Bartimaeus to him. "Come on, Bartimaeus," they said. "Jesus wants to see you."

✂ *Cut figure from C to D.*

How do you think Bartimaeus felt when Jesus wanted to see him? How would you feel if Jesus asked to see you? *Let children respond.*

Bartimaeus came to Jesus as quickly as he could. Jesus asked him, "What do you want?"

"I want to be able to see," said Bartimaeus.

△ *Unfold the figure.*

"All right," said Jesus. "Because you believe in me, you may go and be well."

△ *Fold figure's eyelids out.*

Suddenly, Bartimaeus could see. And the first person he saw was Jesus.

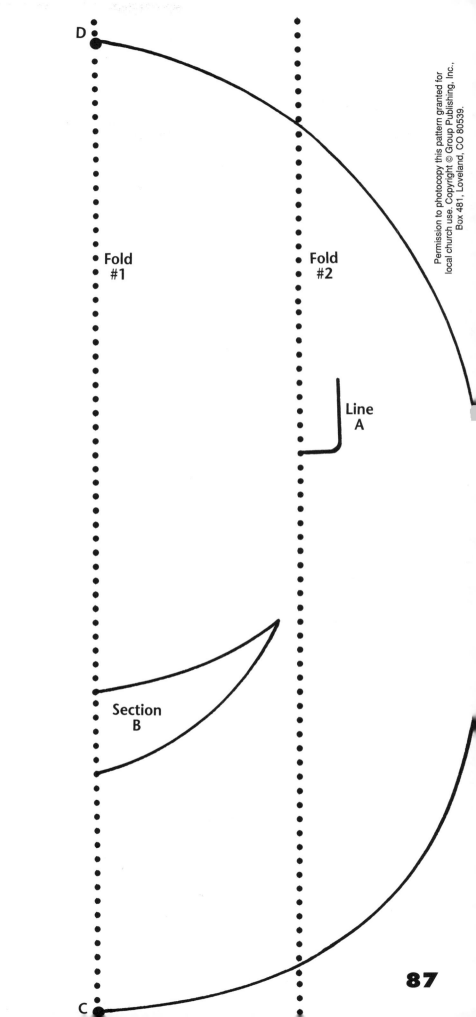

D

Fold
#1

Fold
#2

Line
A

Section
B

C

THE TEN LEPERS

PREPARATION

You'll need transparent tape, scissors, and four sheets of typing paper. Copy the pattern onto one sheet. Lay the sheets of typing paper end to end and tape them together. As you tell the story, you'll be folding the paper accordion-style into 20 panels. Mark off the places where you'll fold the paper.

THE STORY

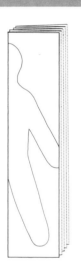

△ Begin folding the paper as you tell the first paragraph. Make sure the pattern is on top.

There were once ten men who had a very bad skin sickness called leprosy. Other people didn't want to catch this sickness, so they made the men live alone outside the city. They couldn't see their friends or their families. How would you feel if you couldn't see your friends or family? *Let children respond.*

One day, Jesus was passing by. The men with leprosy found out that Jesus was coming. So they stood back a little way and called to him. "Jesus! Jesus!"

✂ Cut figure from A to B.

Why did the sick men stand back from Jesus? *Let children respond.*

Jesus knew why they were standing back. He knew they were sick. He said, "Go to the temple and show your skin to the priest."

✂ Cut figure from C to D.

The ten men started walking toward the city. As they were walking, they looked down and saw that their skin was healed.

✂ Cut figure from D to E.

△ Begin unfolding the figure and counting the men. Ask the children to help you count.

One was healed. Two were healed. Three, four, five, six, seven were healed. Eight and nine were healed. Ten were healed. How do you think they felt when they saw that their sickness was gone? *Let children respond.*

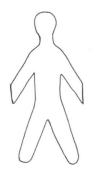

The men who were healed all hurried on their way. All except for one man.

✂ Cut the last man off of the group.

This man stopped. He turned around and went back to find Jesus. He praised God and kneeled down at Jesus' feet. He thanked Jesus for healing him.

What can you remember to thank Jesus for? *Let children respond.*

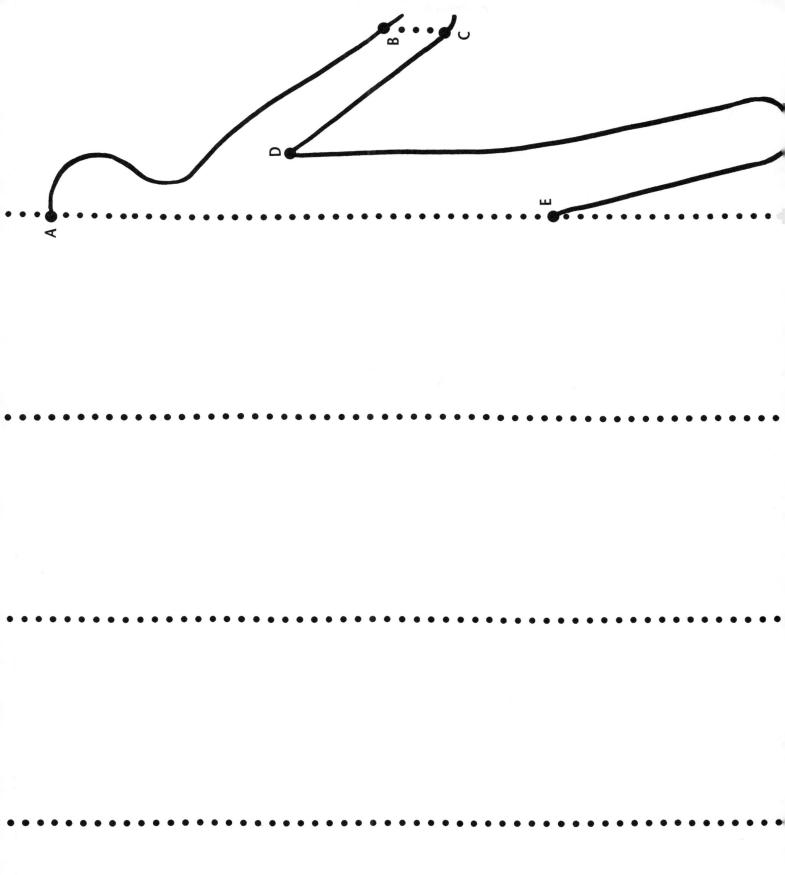

THE WISE MAN'S HOUSE

PREPARATION

You'll need scissors and two sheets of typing paper.
The pattern for this activity is on page 92.

THE STORY

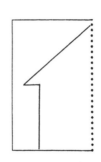

Jesus said that whoever listens to him is like a wise man who built his house on a rock.

△ *Fold one sheet of paper in half horizontally.*

This man found a place to build his house that was on big, flat, sturdy rocks.

✂ *Cut figure from A to B.*

He brought his wood to those rocks and built his house. After he finished building, he moved into the house.

✂ *Cut figure from B to C.*

One day a big, big storm came.

✂ *Cut figure from C to D.*

△ *Unfold the figure.*

The wind shook the house.

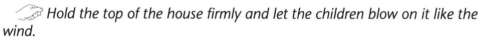 *Hold the top of the house firmly and let the children blow on it like the wind.*

The rain pounded down on the house.

Have the children pat the floor lightly with their palms to make rain sounds.

The water rose up all around the bottom of the house. But the house stayed right where it was. Why didn't the house fall down or float away? *Let children respond.*

The house didn't fall because it was built on strong, steady rock.

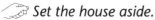 *Set the house aside.*

Jesus said that whoever doesn't listen to him and obey him is like a foolish man who built his house on sand.

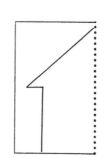

△ *Fold the second sheet of paper in half horizontally.*

✂ *Cut figure from A to B.*

He brought his wood to the sand, and he built his house. After he finished building, he moved into the house.

✂ *Cut figure from B to C.*

One day a big, big storm came.

✂ *Cut figure from C to D.*

 *Unfold the figure.*

The wind shook the house.

☞ *Hold the house and let the children blow on it like the wind.*

The rain pounded down on the house.

Let the children pat the floor to make rain sounds.

The water rose up all around the bottom of the house and washed away that sand. What do you think happened to that man's house? *Let children respond.*

☞ *Shake the house.*

The house creaked and groaned and came crashing down!

☞ *Crumple the paper house.*

Which house would you rather have? Would you rather be a wise person or a foolish person? *Let children respond.*

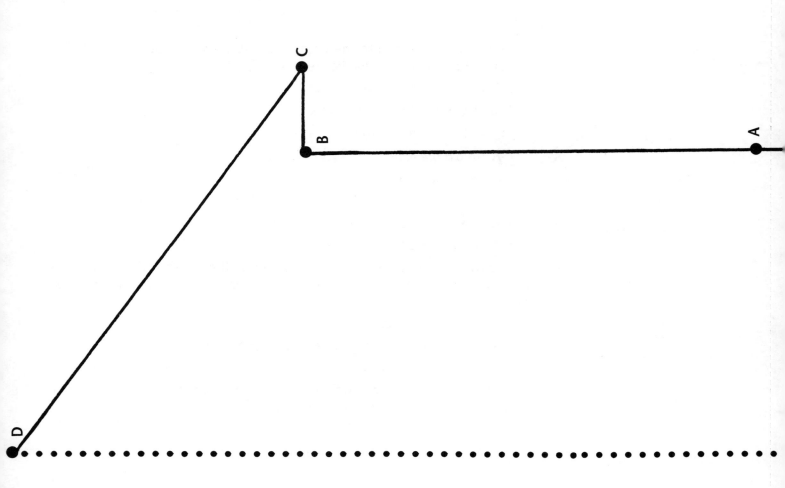

JAIRUS' DAUGHTER

You'll need scissors, a marker, and one sheet of pink construction paper. The pattern for this activity is on page 95.

THE STORY

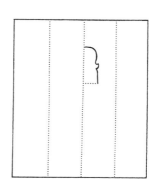

△ *Fold the paper in half vertically.*

One day a man named Jairus came to see Jesus. Jairus was very upset because his little girl was very, very sick. In fact, she was so sick, he thought she might die. Why do you think Jairus went to see Jesus? *Let children respond.*

Jairus kneeled down in front of Jesus. "Please come heal my little girl," he said. So Jesus went with him.

✂ *Cut figure along line A.*

Before they reached Jairus' house, some men met them on the road. "It's too late," they told Jairus. "Your daughter has died. You can let Jesus go on and do other things now." How would you feel if you found out someone in your family had died? *Let children respond.*

△ *Open up the figure and fold each side toward the center.*

But Jesus said to Jairus, "Don't worry. Just believe." And Jesus kept walking with Jairus to his house.

When they got there, many people were standing around crying about the little girl who had died. Jesus told them, "She's not dead. She's just asleep." Do you think those people believed Jesus? *Let children respond.*

They didn't believe the little girl was really alive. They laughed at Jesus. How do you think Jesus felt when those people laughed at him? *Let children respond.*

△ *Unfold the sides of the figure halfway and set the paper on a table or floor so it becomes the little girl's bed.*

Jesus went into the girl's room. He saw her lying on her bed. And he said to her, "Little girl, get up."

The little girl opened her eyes.

☞ *Draw eyes and a smile on the figure in bed.*

She stood up and walked around.

93

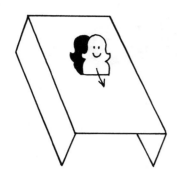

Bend the figure to sit up in bed.

The little girl was just fine. Jesus had made her well again.

Fold #2 →

Fold #1 →

Fold #3 →

Line A

Fold back ←

Fold back →

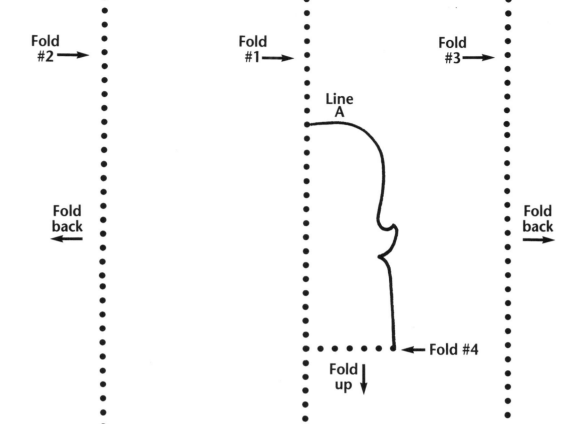

← **Fold #4**

Fold up ↓

ZACCHAEUS

You'll need scissors and one sheet of green construction paper.
The pattern for this activity is on page 98.

THE STORY

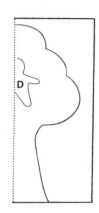

△ *Fold the paper in half vertically.*

Zacchaeus was a tax collector. People had to give him money to give to the king. But Zacchaeus didn't give all of the people's money to the king. Zacchaeus kept some of the money for himself, and he got very rich. The people weren't happy about this. How would you feel if someone was taking your money? *Let children respond.*

Most of the people didn't like Zacchaeus. They didn't like him one bit.

Jesus was coming to the town where Zacchaeus lived. Everyone in town went out to the road where Jesus would pass. They wanted to see and hear Jesus. What would you do if Jesus came to our town? *Let children respond.*

✂ *Cut figure from A to B.*

Zacchaeus followed the crowds of people. But he couldn't find a place to stand where he could see.

✂ *Cut figure from B to C.*

Zacchaeus was a very short man, and everyone else was standing in front of him. Have you ever tried to see over a crowd of people? What was it like? *Let children respond.*

No one would let Zacchaeus get through so he could see.

✂ *Cut out section D, leaving a small portion attached at the top.*

Then Zacchaeus saw a tall tree nearby. So guess what he did. He climbed up in the tree so he could see over all the people.

△ *Open the figure to show Zacchaeus in the tree.*

The tree was a perfect place to watch Jesus pass. Soon Zacchaeus could see Jesus coming. When Jesus got close to the tree where Zacchaeus was, he looked up at Zacchaeus. He said, "Come down, Zacchaeus. I want to come over to your house and spend some time with you." How would it feel if you were Zacchaeus and Jesus found you in a tree? *Let children respond.*

Zacchaeus was surprised. But he came down quickly.

Gently and quickly tear off the Zacchaeus figure and bring him down from the tree.

Zacchaeus and Jesus walked together to his house. As he was talking to Jesus, Zacchaeus decided to change his ways. He said, "I'll pay back all the money that I took from the people." How do you think Jesus felt when Zacchaeus decided to give the money back? *Let children respond.*

Jesus said, "Zacchaeus, this is a great day, because you have decided to do what's right."

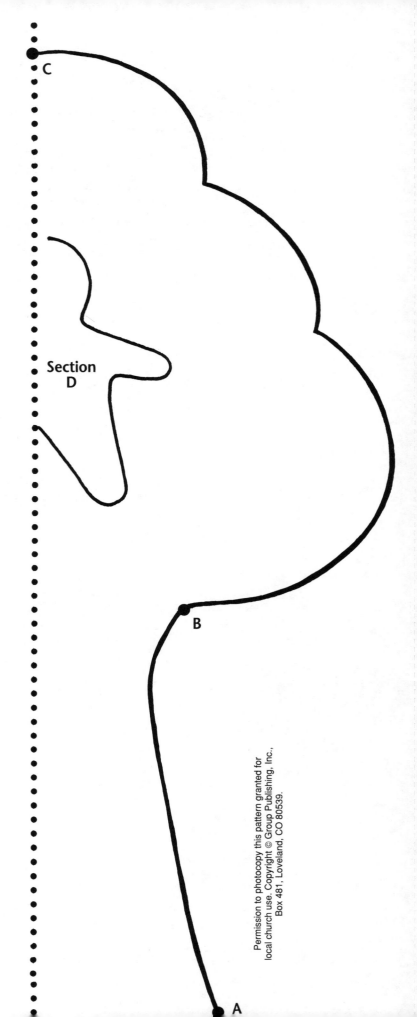

C

Section
D

B

A

JESUS, THE KING ON A COLT

PREPARATION

You'll need scissors and a large sheet of green construction paper. The pattern for this activity is on page 101.

THE STORY

△ *Fold the paper in half vertically.*

Jesus walked many places. But one day he decided to ride. Did he ride in a bus or a car? Did he ride on an animal? What kind of animal? *Let children respond.*

Jesus wanted to ride a young donkey to Jerusalem. Do you know what a young donkey is called? *Let children respond.*

A young donkey is called a colt. Jesus asked two of his friends to go into a little village and look for a colt that no one had ever ridden before.

✂ *Cut figure from A to B.*

Jesus said they'd find a colt tied in the village, and they were supposed to untie it and bring it to Jesus. Jesus said, "If anyone asks you what you're doing, tell them the Lord needs this colt."

✂ *Cut figure from B to C.*

So Jesus' two friends did what Jesus asked. They went to the village. They found the colt tied there, and they untied it.

✂ *Cut figure from C to D.*

But someone asked them what they were doing. What had Jesus told them to say? *Let children respond.*

"The Lord needs this colt," they said. Then the people let them take the colt.

✂ *Cut figure from D to E.*

Jesus' friends brought him the colt. They put their coats on the colt's back to make a saddle.

✂ *Cut figure from E to F.*

Jesus' friends helped Jesus get on. Then they started out on the road to Jerusalem.

✂ *Cut figure from F to G.*

The people they met on the way spread their coats over the road. They cut palm branches off the trees.

✂ *Cut figure from G to H.*

They put some branches on the road and waved other branches.

△ *Unfold the figure and wave it.*

Why did the people put their branches and coats on the road? *Let children respond.*

The people called out, "Blessed is the one who comes in the Lord's name! Peace and glory! Hosanna! Hosanna!"

The people with the coats and branches wanted to show Jesus how happy they were to see him and how much they loved him. What can you do to show Jesus how much you love him? *Let children respond.*

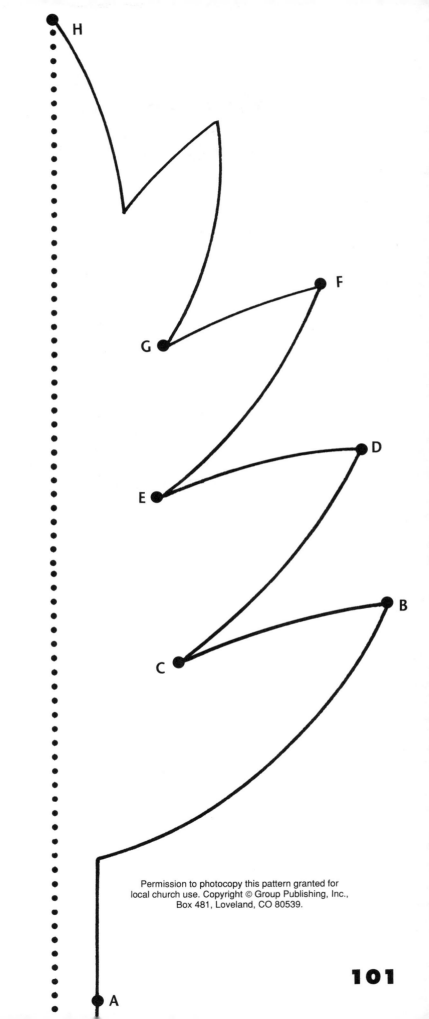

H

F

G

D

E

B

C

A

PETER AND JOHN HEAL A LAME MAN

PREPARATION

You'll need scissors and one sheet of typing paper.

THE STORY

Fold the paper in half vertically.

At three o'clock one afternoon, Peter and John went to the temple to pray. There was a man who couldn't walk sitting at the gate of the temple. He was sitting by the gate called the Beautiful Gate. Why do you think he was sitting there? What do you think he was doing? *Let children respond.*

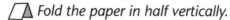Fold the paper accordion-style horizontally from the bottom up to dotted line A.

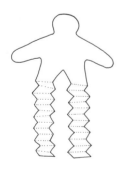

Line A

The man was begging people for money. When Peter and John walked by this man, he asked them for money, too.

Peter said, "I don't have any money to give you, but I have something else to give you. In Jesus' name, get up and walk."

Which do you think the man would rather have: the money or the ability to walk? *Let children respond.*

Cut the figure as shown. Be sure to cut through your accordion fold.

Peter reached down and took the man's hand.

Unfold the figure and hold it up.

Make the man jump and leap.

He helped the man get up. And the man began to walk. In fact, the man began to jump and praise God, because he was so happy he'd been healed. What do you do to praise God when you're happy? *Let children respond.*

The man jumped and leaped all the way into the temple. The people in the temple recognized this man. They knew he couldn't walk. They knew he'd been begging at the temple gate. What do you think they thought when they saw him jumping around? *Let children respond.*

All the people were amazed by what had happened.

Peter said, "Why are you amazed? We didn't make this man well. Jesus made him well."

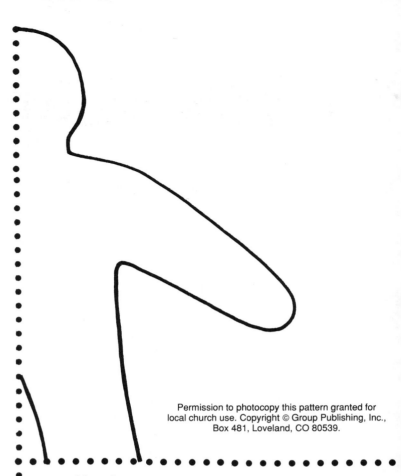

Line A

PETER IS RESCUED

PREPARATION

You'll need scissors and one sheet of yellow construction paper.
The pattern for this activity is on page 106.

THE STORY

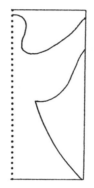

△ *Fold the paper in half vertically.*

The leaders of the country didn't like to hear about Jesus. They didn't believe Jesus was God's son. They didn't want anyone to teach about Jesus. So when they heard Peter teaching other people about Jesus, they put Peter in jail.

One night, while Peter was in jail, asleep between two soldiers, God sent an angel to help him. The angel woke Peter up. What do you think Peter thought? How would you feel if an angel woke you up? *Let children respond.*

The angel said, "Hurry! Put on your clothes and sandals and follow me!" Peter did what the angel said.

✂ *Cut figure from A to B.*

The angel led Peter past all the guards. They went to the iron gate that led to the city. The gate opened for them all by itself, and they went out into the city streets. They walked down one street, and then the angel left.

✂ *Cut figure from B to C.*

What do you think Peter did after the angel left? Where did he go? *Let children respond.*

Peter hurried to the house where his friend John Mark's mother lived. Many of his friends were there praying for him. Peter knocked on the door.

✂ *Cut figure from D to E.*

A servant girl named Rhoda asked, "Who's there?" When Peter answered, she recognized his voice. What do you think Rhoda did after she heard Peter's voice? *Let children respond.*

Rhoda was so surprised that she didn't let Peter in! She ran to tell the others that Peter was at the door. What would you do if you were Rhoda? What would you think if you were one of Peter's friends? *Let children respond.*

✂ *Cut figure from E to F.*

None of the friends believed Rhoda. But Peter kept on knocking until they

finally let him in. Then he told them everything that had happened. He told them about the gates opening by themselves and about the special messenger God sent to help him.

△ *Unfold the figure.*

Peter and his friends all praised and thanked God together.

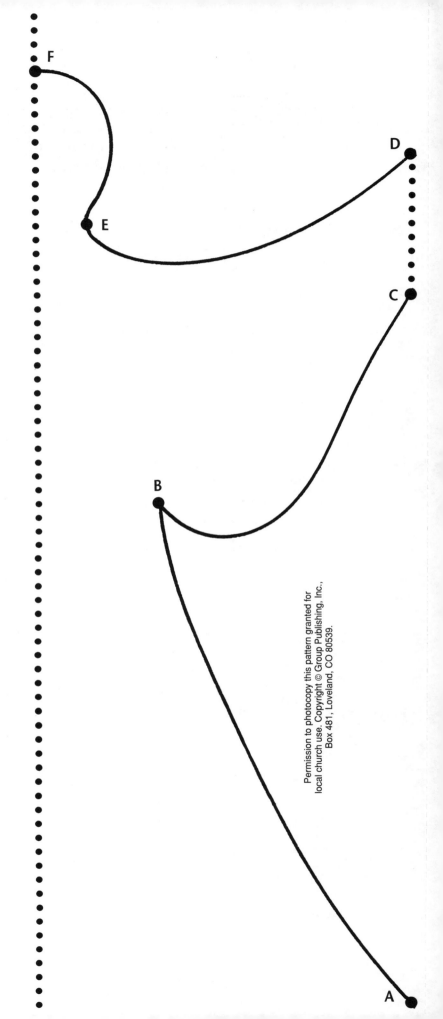

F

D

E

C

B

A

PAUL AND SILAS IN JAIL

PREPARATION

You'll need scissors and one sheet of typing paper.
The pattern for this activity is on page 109.

THE STORY

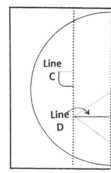

Line C

Line D

/△ *Fold the paper in half horizontally.*

✄ *Cut figure from A to B.*

Paul and Silas were teaching about Jesus. But some people didn't like what they were doing. So they locked Paul and Silas in jail.

/△ *Fold paper in half again and cut along line C.*

Paul and Silas knew that God was still with them, even in jail.

/△ *Unfold figure halfway and cut along line D.*

☞ *With index finger, pull section E outside the figure and crease.*

☞ *With index finger, pull section F outside the figure and crease.*

Paul and Silas prayed. They sang songs to God.

/△ *Unfold the figure.*

☞ *Make the mouth "sing" by carefully pulling and pushing the sides of the head.*

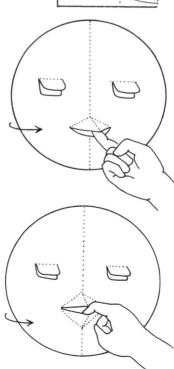

What do you think the other people in jail thought about Paul and Silas' praying and singing? *Let children respond.*

Very late one night, while Paul and Silas were singing and praying, the ground began to shake with an earthquake. The earthquake was so strong that all the jail doors popped open. The chains on all the prisoners broke off. How would you feel if you were a prisoner and your chains broke off? What would you do? How would feel if you were the jailer guarding those prisoners? *Let children respond.*

The jailer was very upset. He thought all the prisoners would run away, and he'd be in trouble for letting them escape.

But Paul and Silas called to him and said, "Don't worry. We're all still here."

The jailer brought lights to see for himself. It was true.

All the prisoners was there. "What should I do?" he asked Paul and Silas.

What do you think he should do? *Let children respond.*

Paul and Silas told him, "You should believe in Jesus." Then they told the jailer and his family about Jesus. The jailer and his family listened and decided to believe in Jesus. The whole family was baptized. And they were all filled with joy.

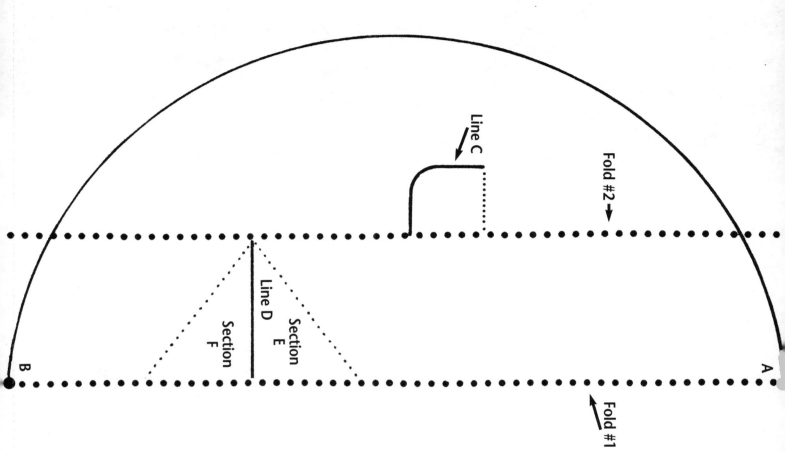

Line C

Fold #2 →

B

A

Line D

Section E

Section F

Fold #1 ↑

For more amazing resources

visit us at
group.com...

...or call us at
1-800-447-1070!

Group
Incredible things will happen